LOWFAT
INTERNATIONAL CUISINE

Jane Rubey

A Nitty Gritty® Cookbook

Printed in the United States of America.

ISBN 0-911954-92-9

Production Consultant:
   Vicki L. Crampton
Photographer: Kathryn Opp
Food Stylist:
   Carol Cooper Ladd
Assistant to Food Stylist:
   Barbara Brooks
Illustrator: Carol Webb Atherly

   For their cooperation in sharing props and locations for use in photographs, we extend special thanks to Cindy Arnold, Mary Hoeflick, Dolores Pranger and Deb Norby.

Table of Contents

METRIC CONVERSION CHART

Liquid or Dry Measuring Cup (based on an 8 ounce cup)
1/4 cup = 60 ml
1/3 cup = 80 ml
1/2 cup = 125 ml
3/4 cup = 190 ml
1 cup = 250 ml
2 cups = 500 ml

Liquid or Dry Measuring Cup (based on a 10 ounce cup)
1/4 cup = 80 ml
1/3 cup = 100 ml
1/2 cup = 150 ml
3/4 cup = 230 ml
1 cup = 300 ml
2 cups = 600 ml

Liquid or Dry Teaspoon and Tablespoon
1/4 tsp. = 1.5 ml
1/2 tsp. = 3 ml
1 tsp. = 5 ml
3 tsp. = 1 tbs. = 15 ml

Temperatures

°F	=	°C
200	=	100
250	=	120
275	=	140
300	=	150
325	=	160
350	=	180
375	=	190
400	=	200
425	=	220
450	=	230
475	=	240
500	=	260
550	=	280

Pan Sizes (1 inch = 25mm)
8-inch pan (round or square) = 200 mm x 200 mm
9-inch pan (round or square) = 225 mm x 225 mm
9 x 5 x 3-inch loaf pan = 225 mm x 125 mm x 75 mm
1/4 inch thickness = 5 mm
1/8 inch thickness = 2.5 mm

Pressure Cooker
100 Kpa = 15 pounds per square inch
70 Kpa = 10 pounds per square inch
35 Kpa = 5 pounds per square inch

Mass
1 ounce = 30 g
4 ounces = 1/4 pound = 125 g
8 ounces = 1/2 pounds = 250 g
16 ounces = 1 pound = 500 g
2 pounds = 1 kg

Key   (America uses an 8 ounce cup — Britain uses a 10 ounce cup)

ml = milliliter
l = liter
g = gram
K = Kilo (one thousand)
mm = millimeter
m = mill (a thousandth)
°F = degrees Fahrenheit

°C = degrees Celsius
tsp. = teaspoon
tbs. = tablespoon
Kpa = (pounds pressure per square inch)
      This configuration is used for pressure
      cookers only.

Metric equivalents are rounded to conform to existing metric measuring utensils.

Introduction

Adventures in good eating can combine the pleasures of taste, texture and aroma with the quest for healthful, nutritious food. This international collection of recipes does just that. Fats are restricted and modified; fibers are encouraged. As a direct result, calories decrease, yielding light, lean cuisine.

Lean Cuisine

Modifying fat intake has two different meanings. First, it is important to reduce the **overall amount of fat** in the diet. Fats are associated with many diseases, in particular heart disease, cancer, stroke and diabetes. The average American diet could benefit by cutting out one-third to one-half of the calories supplied by fats, a shift from the current consumption of 40% of total daily calories as fats to a leaner 20% to 25%.

Replacement calories would come from fiber-rich, complex carbohydrate foods such as whole grains, legumes, vegetables and fruits. When you eat right, you eat light. Since carbohydrates have less than half as many calories as fats, ounce for ounce, you fill up before you fatten up.

When selecting foods and planning menus, emphasize complex carbohydrates with fibers and minimize fats. For example, start the day with a nonfat breakfast: wholegrain cereal or bread, nonfat milk, fruit and beverage without added fat.

Throughout the day,
- focus on bean, grain and vegetable entrees,
- emphasize plant proteins in preference to animal proteins,
- use meats and cheeses as condiments,
- limit eggs to their essential role as an ingredient,
- dress up foods with nuts and seeds, and
- enjoy fruits as sweets.

The second meaning of modifying fat intake has to do with **different forms of fats** in foods. Some are ``better;'' some are ``worse.''

Saturated fats. Saturated fats are hard at room temperature and offer no nutrition, only ``empty,'' ``fattening,'' concentrated calories. Furthermore, saturated fats encourage the body to make additional cholesterol, elevating the serum cholesterol level. **Hydrogenation** is a process by which fats are made saturated. Coconut oil, palm oil, animal fats (including cheese, butter, lard and meats), margarine and shortening contain saturated fats.

Polyunsaturated fats. These fats are liquid at room temperature and are equally ``fattening.'' In addition, they are susceptible to oxidation or rancidity (**always** refrigerate unsaturated fats!) which encourages cancer. Safflower, sunflower, cottonseed, corn and soy oils are commonly available polyunsaturated fats.

We need a very small amount of one particular polyunsaturated fatty acid as a nutrient; this is readily available in the typical diet. Recent evidence has demonstrated the importance of several other polyunsaturated fatty acids (omega-3's) found primarily in fish oil. The need for these can be met best by consuming several servings of coldwater fish weekly.

Monounsaturated fats. These fats are also liquid at room temperature and "fattening," and appear to be least harmful. Always remembering that total fat intake, whether saturated or unsaturated, needs to be sharply controlled, the mono-unsaturates are the better choice if fat is necessary. Olive oil and canola oil*, a relative newcomer to the food scene, are highly monounsaturated. Peanut oil, a fairly even mixture of monounsaturates and polyunsaturates, offers an additional choice.

Most food fats contain a mixture of the three forms of fat. We designate the food fat as one type or another depending upon which form of fat predominates. For example, olive oil is 77% monounsaturated, 14% saturated and 9% polyunsaturated. Hence olive oil is said to be "monounsaturated." Peanut oil, 48% monounsaturated, is also classified as monounsaturated, although further down the list. Lard, composed fairly evenly of two types of fat, 41% saturated and 47% monounsaturated, is listed twice.

The American Heart Association recommends a balance of the various types of fats so that less than one-third of fats eaten are saturated, less than one-third are polyunsaturated and the remaining fats are monounsaturated. To effect this, routinely avoid hard fats and animal fats. Shift to monounsaturated oils for salad dressings and cooking oils. Bake with monounsaturates when possible. This is not to suggest that cheese, butter, mayonnaise or other foods with undesirable fats should never be consumed. It does indicate, however, that their use be limited and specific to those

*derived from rapeseed; sold under labels such as Puritan and Spectrum.

occasions when they truly make a difference. For example, a little grated cheese on top of a tostada adds a unique, crowning touch; but limit the amount and save cheese for a two- or three-times-per-month treat.

Predominant Form of Fat in Food Fat Sources

(listed in order of decreasing percentage)

Monounsaturated	Polyunsaturated	Saturated
Olive	Safflower	Coconut
Avocado	Grapeseed	Palm kernel
Canola (rapeseed)	Sunflower	Butter
Almond	Wheat germ	Palm
Salmon	Corn	Beef
Egg yolk	Soybean	Mutton
Peanut	Cottonseed	Chicken
Margarine (varies)	Cod liver	Lard
Chicken	Walnut	Egg yolk
Lard	Mayonnaise (varies)	Shortening (varies)
Sesame	Margarine (varies)	Chocolate

Lighter Recipes

The total amount of fat in a recipe can often be reduced without negating the original intent of the dish. The recipes in this collection have been modified to contain less total fat. You can modify your own favorite recipes in the same way. Evaluate the purpose of the fat and attempt to substitute a nonfat replacement or reduce the overall amount or both. Good nonstick cookware facilitates lowfat cooking. Try the following:

Instead of **Higher Fat**	Use **Lower Fat**
Whole or lowfat milk*	Nonfat milk
Whole or lowfat yogurt	Nonfat yogurt
Cream, half and half	Evaporated skim milk; nonfat milk with nonfat milk powder added
Creamed cottage cheese	Lowfat or nonfat cottage cheese
Sour cream	Yogurt
Cream cheese	Yogurt cheese (see page 46)
Gelato, ice cream	Ice milk, sherbet, sorbet
Full fat cheeses	Part skim mozzarella, ricotta
Whole egg	2 egg whites; egg substitute; reduced-cholesterol egg
Regular meats	Extra-lean meats; trimmed
Red meats, poultry with skin	Fish, shellfish; skinless chicken, turkey; rabbit
Fish canned in oil	Fish canned in water
Store-bought baked goods	Home-baked goods made with monounsaturated fat
Regular crackers, chips	Rye crisp bread; pretzels
Regular roasted nuts, seeds	Dry roasted nuts, seeds
1 cup hard, saturated fat	7/8 cup liquid, monounsaturated fat
Mayonnaise on sandwich	Mustard, catsup
Mayonnaise made with polyunsaturated fat	Mayonnaise made with monounsaturated fat
Butter, margarine on toast	Peanut butter; yogurt cheese; jam
Hydrogenated peanut butter	Natural peanut butter
Butter, margarine in baking	Light olive or canola oil
Fat-based sauce	Water-based sauce
Chocolate	Cocoa

*Lowfat milk contains 1 tsp. butterfat per cup. Assuming consumption of 2 cups per day, this adds up to about 7.5 pounds of butter over one year. Double this to 15 pounds per year of hidden butterfat if drinking whole milk!

Nutrient Analysis

This book offers the added advantage of nutritional information given for each recipe. This is based on the most current data available from the USDA*. The analysis is presented for a single serving or a specified amount such as per cookie. Optional ingredients are not included. If a choice of ingredients is given, the one listed first is used in the calculation. Recipes using stock or broth assume canned, salted broth.

Use the nutritional information to evaluate fat content. Examine total fat grams in relation to the suggested daily limit of 50 grams. In addition, notice the distribution across the various forms of fat. The specified use of olive or canola oil in many of the recipes enhances the monounsaturated proportion and restricts the others. Substituting other fats will change the profile. Meats vary in fat content and change during preparation; values for cooked meat dishes can only approximate food composition.

Fiber values are boosted, when possible, by the use of wholegrains such as brown rice and whole wheat flour. For best results, be sure the flour is finely ground.

Cholesterol values appear whenever animal foods are used. (Plant foods have no cholesterol.) The American Heart Association suggests limiting cholesterol intake to 100 mg per 1000 calories. Remember: saturated fats have a much greater effect on elevating serum cholesterol than does the actual cholesterol you eat.

Sodium and potassium values are both given. It is the balanced intake of this mineral team that is important.

*Recipes analyzed using **The Food Processor II**, available from ESHA Research, P.O. Box 13028, Salem, OR 97309.

Africa

The cuisine of Africa is as varied as its many cultures. The South African bredie and bobotie reflect the Dutch presence at the Cape. Couscous, a culinary tradition in North Africa, is eaten throughout the Arab world.

Peanut Millet Soup (Groundnut Soup)
East Africa

Peanuts contribute most of the fat in this elegant soup, boosting its monosaturation. Combine with a lightly dressed tossed green salad for a complete meal.

3 cups chicken stock, preferably homemade
   (see **Chicken and Stock,** page 28)
1 cup onion, chopped (1 medium onion)
1 cup leek, chopped (1 medium leek including 2" of green top, pulled apart,
   washed thoroughly, and cut into quarters lengthwise)
1 cup carrot, chopped (2 medium carrots, peeled)
⅓ cup millet, raw **or** rice
½ tsp. salt
½ cup natural smooth peanut butter
cayenne pepper to taste
dry roasted peanuts, chopped (optional)

In a large saucepan, combine stock, onion, leek and carrot and bring to a boil. Reduce heat, cover and simmer 20 minutes or until vegetables are completely cooked. Separate vegetables from broth using a colander or sieve. Puree vegetables in a food processor or blender. Return broth and pureed vegetables to saucepan and bring to a boil. Add millet and salt. Reduce heat to simmer and cook, covered, 20 minutes. In a small bowl, whisk together about one cup of soup and peanut butter. Add to soup. Season to taste. Serve hot, garnished with chopped peanuts, if desired.

Nutritional information per serving   158 calories, 9.1 grams fat, 1.2 grams saturated fat, 2.7 grams polyunsaturated fat, 4.3 grams monounsaturated fat, 8 grams protein, 14 grams carbohydrate, 2.3 grams fiber, 0 mg cholesterol, 436 mg sodium, 336 mg potassium

Meat and Vegetable Stew with Semolina (Couscous)
North Africa

Servings: 6

Couscous refers both to a stew and a grain dish. Couscous, the grain, is a medium-grind semolina, the center portion of the grain of wheat. This can be served by itself as a side dish as you would use rice or noodles. Couscous, the stew, is popular throughout the various countries of North Africa with each area seasoning the dish uniquely. Algeria adds tomato; Tunisia uses additional spice and chili pepper; Morocco flavors with saffron. The stew is served surrounded by the grain on a large platter.

½ lb. boneless leg of lamb **or** tender beef, trimmed of all fat, cut into 1" cubes
1 tbs. canola oil
1 cup onion, cut into narrow wedges (1 medium onion)
1 carrot, peeled, cut into ¾" pieces
1 turnip, peeled, cut into ¾" cubes
1 bay leaf
1 clove garlic, minced
¼ tsp. ginger

¼ tsp. cumin
1 tsp. ground coriander
½ tsp. salt
¼ tsp. hot red pepper flakes
1½ cups water **or** broth
1 green pepper, cut into 1" squares
1 zucchini, cut into ¾" slices
1 (15 ozs.) can garbanzo beans **or** 1½ cups cooked, drained
1 tbs. flour
¼ cup water

In a large pan, brown meat in oil. Add onion, carrot and turnip along with seasonings and water. Cook, covered, 10 minutes. Add remaining vegetables and garbanzo beans. Cook, partially covered, another 10 minutes. Mix flour with water and add to stew; cook, stirring, 2 more minutes. Serve with **Steamed Semolina** (couscous grain), page 12.

Nutritional information per serving   192 calories, 6.7 grams fat, 1.5 grams saturated fat, 1.4 grams polyunsaturated fat, 2.9 grams monounsaturated fat, 15 grams protein, 18 grams carbohydrate, 3.9 grams fiber, 34 mg cholesterol, 229 mg sodium, 449 mg potassium

Steamed Semolina (Couscous)
Africa

And here we have couscous, the grain.

2¼ cups water
¾ tsp. salt
1 tbs. butter
1 (10 ozs.) pkg. couscous (medium-grind semolina)
½ cup raisins, preferably golden

Bring water to a boil in a large saucepan. Add salt, butter, couscous and raisins. Remove from heat and let stand 5 minutes until water is absorbed and grain fluffy. Mound on a heated platter. Make a well in the center of the mound and fill with **Couscous Stew**, page 10.

Nutritional information per serving   221 calories, 2.8 grams fat, 1.4 grams saturated fat, 0.4 grams polyunsaturated fat, 0.7 grams monounsaturated fat, 5 grams protein, 46 grams carbohydrate, 1.1 grams fiber, 5 mg cholesterol, 287 mg sodium, 158 mg potassium

---

Stewed Okra
Africa

This dish has made its way from Africa to South America, the Caribbean and the southern United States.

2 tsp. peanut oil
1 cup onion, finely chopped
2 cups tomato, chopped **or**
   2 cups canned tomatoes with juice
1 fresh hot chili pepper, minced **or**
   1 tsp. canned or bottled

2 cloves garlic, minced
½ tsp. salt
freshly ground pepper
¾ lb. fresh okra, ends trimmed

In a large skillet with a lid, sauté onion in oil until soft but not browned. Add tomatoes, chili, garlic, salt and pepper and cook, stirring, about 5 minutes. Add okra pods and push them into the mixture to coat them. Cover and simmer vegetables for about 20 minutes, until okra is tender when pierced with the tip of a sharp knife. Serve hot.

Nutritional information per serving   81 calories, 2.7 grams fat, 0.5 grams saturated fat, 0.9 grams polyunsaturated fat, 1.1 grams monounsaturated fat, 3 grams protein, 14 grams carbohydrate, 4 grams fiber, 0 mg cholesterol, 289 mg sodium, 534 mg potassium

◄ **Chinese Chicken Salad (page 26)**

Lamb and Green Bean Stew
(Green Bean Bredie)
Servings: 6
South Africa

Bredies are stews usually made with lamb, onions, chilies and a predominant vegetable such as cauliflower, cabbage, tomatoes, pumpkin or green beans, as in this case. Traditionally they are served with rice.

¾ lb. boneless leg of lamb **or** shoulder, all fat removed, cut into ¾" squares
1 cup onion, chopped
1 clove garlic, minced
1 tsp. fresh ginger root, peeled, minced
1 cup water
1 lb. fresh green beans, ends trimmed, cut into 1" lengths **or** 2 (9 ozs. each) pkgs. frozen cut green beans
1 lb. boiling potatoes (2 medium), diced
1 tsp.-1 tbs. fresh hot chili, seeds removed, minced*
½ tsp. thyme
1 tsp. salt
freshly ground pepper

In a large, heavy-bottomed saucepan, brown meat, stirring to prevent burning. When richly browned, after about 10 minutes, add onion, garlic and ginger. Cook until onions are soft and translucent. Add water, beans, potato and seasonings. Heat to boiling, cover, reduce heat and simmer, stirring occasionally, for 45 to 60 minutes or until meat is tender.

Nutritional information per serving 225 calories, 5 grams fat, 2 grams saturated fat, 0.5 grams polyunsaturated fat, 1.7 grams monounsaturated fat, 19 grams protein, 26 grams carbohydrate, 3.9 grams fiber, 51 mg cholesterol, 403 mg sodium, 803 mg potassium

*To Handle Fresh Chilies: use care; the volatile oils in chilies can irritate the skin. Protect sensitive hands with rubber gloves; be careful not to touch face or eyes. Retain some seeds if additional ''heat'' is desired.

Baked Lamb Curry (Bobotie)
South Africa

Servings: 8

Curry was brought to South Africa from the Far East by sailors rounding the Cape. It has been enjoyed in dishes such as this for many years.

2 slices white bread, crusts removed
  (sourdough is nice)
1 cup nonfat milk
1 lb. extra-lean ground lamb
1 lb. ground turkey
1½ cups onion, chopped
1 clove garlic, minced
2 tbs. curry powder
1 tbs. brown sugar

1 tsp. salt
freshly ground pepper
¼ cup fresh lemon juice (one lemon)
1 cup apple, cored, shredded
½ cup raisins
¼ cup almonds*, chopped, toasted
1 egg white, beaten
2 eggs

In a small bowl, soak bread in milk. In a large skillet, brown lamb and turkey; remove meat to a very large bowl using a slotted spoon. Discard all fat. (A gravy separator works nicely for this.) Cook onion in remaining meat juices until soft. Add garlic, curry, sugar, salt and pepper and mix well. Add onion and

18 Africa

seasonings to meat in bowl. Separate bread from milk using a sieve. Squeeze bread "dry;" reserve all milk. Add bread along with lemon, apple, raisins, almonds and egg white to meat and mix thoroughly. Turn into a greased 3-quart high-sided casserole, pressing well and smoothing top. Beat eggs with reserved milk; pour on top of meat. Bake at 300° for 50 to 60 minutes or until completely hot and custard on top is set. This is traditionally served with rice.

Nutritional information per serving   390 calories, 16.6 grams fat, 5.2 grams saturated fat, 3 grams polyunsaturated fat, 7.2 grams monounsaturated fat, 36 grams protein, 25 grams carbohydrate, 2.9 grams fiber, 167 mg cholesterol, 464 mg sodium, 634 mg potassium

* **To Toast Nuts**: spread nuts in a single layer on a large baking sheet (or glass dish for microwave). Place in 375° oven for 5 to 10 minutes (or in microwave at full power for several minutes). Watch closely, turning several times to prevent scorching. When properly toasted, nuts will give off a rich aroma and be lightly browned. If toasting unblanched almonds, break open a nut and look for a lightly browned interior.

Cardamom Cookies (Caramongscraps)
South Africa

36 cookies

Spiced cookies were introduced to South Africa by the early Dutch settlers.

¼ cup butter
½ cup sugar
1 egg
1½ cups whole wheat flour,
  very finely ground **or**
  all-purpose flour
¼ tsp. salt

½ tsp. ground cardamom
1½ tsp. baking powder
¼ cup dried, unsweetened coconut
½ tsp. grated lemon peel
⅓ cup candied ginger, finely chopped
2 tbs. water
sugar

Preheat oven to 350°. Cream butter and sugar together in a large mixer bowl. Add egg and beat until smooth. Sift flour, salt, cardamom and baking powder together, discarding any especially large particles of bran. Add dry ingredients along with coconut, lemon peel and ginger to bowl and blend well. Add water and mix only enough to pull dough together. Divide dough into 36 mounds on nonstick cookie sheets. Using a flat-bottomed glass, stamp each mound flat by dipping glass bottom into sugar in a saucer and flattening cookie. Bake 10 minutes or until edges start to brown lightly. Remove cookies from cookie sheets and cool on a rack. Store in a tin with a tight-fitting lid.

Nutritional information per cookie   50 calories, 1.7 grams fat, 1.1 grams saturated fat, 0.1 grams polyunsaturated fat, 0.5 grams monounsaturated fat, 1 gram protein, 8 grams carbohydrate, 0.6 grams fiber, 11 mg cholesterol, 33 mg sodium, 26 mg potassium

Asia

Chinese cuisine is the oldest and, many would say, the best in the world. Asian meals can run to many courses and, especially in Japan, food becomes art in addition to nourishment.

Fried Rice

China

This is a great way to use up leftover meats and veggies. Just remember to minimize the "fried" part.

1 cup converted white rice
2 cups water
1 tbs. peanut oil **or** canola oil
½ cup green onion, chopped
1 clove garlic, minced
½ cup celery, chopped
½ cup frozen peas, thawed

½ cup extra-lean ham, diced **or** other cooked meat or poultry
1 cup bean sprouts (optional)
1 tbs. rice vinegar
2 tbs. soy sauce
freshly ground pepper
1 egg, beaten

In a medium saucepan, stir rice into water. Bring to a boil; cover; reduce heat to simmer and cook 20 minutes. In a large skillet, heat oil over moderate heat and sauté onion, garlic and celery until soft, about 2 minutes. Add peas, ham, sprouts (if desired) and seasonings and stir well. Remove from heat. Stir in cooked rice and then egg, stirring to blend all ingredients. Serve hot or as a cold salad.

Nutritional information per serving 275 calories, 6.2 grams fat, 1.4 grams saturated fat, 1.5 grams polyunsaturated fat, 2.7 grams monounsaturated fat, 11 grams protein, 43 grams carbohydrate, 2 grams fiber, 79 mg cholesterol, 872 mg sodium, 300 mg potassium

Sour and Hot Soup
China

Servings: 13

This soup combines the nip of vinegar and the heat of Chinese chili oil. It will warm your toes on the coldest of days.

¼ lb. boneless pork, trimmed of all fat
1 qt. chicken stock, preferably homemade (see **Chicken and Stock**, page 28)
3 ozs. fresh shiitake mushrooms **or** 4-6 dried Chinese mushrooms rehydrated
    in warm water for 30 minutes, drained
1 (5 ozs.) can bamboo shoots, drained
6 ozs. firm tofu (soybean curd), diced into ½" pieces
1 tbs. soy sauce
2 tbs. rice vinegar
2 tbs. cornstarch
3 tbs. water
¼ tsp. chili oil*, or to taste, if desired
1 egg, lightly beaten
2 tsp. sesame oil
1 green onion, finely minced

Cut pork into long, thin strips. Brown in a large heavy saucepan. Add stock to pan and heat. Remove tough, woody stems from mushrooms and slice caps thinly. Slice bamboo shoots into thin, long strips. Add mushrooms, bamboo shoots, tofu, soy sauce and vinegar to pan and bring to a boil. In a small bowl, mix cornstarch in water; add to soup and stir until thickened. Season to taste with chili oil. Swirl egg and sesame oil into hot soup. Serve immediately, topped with green onion.

Nutritional information per ½ cup serving   68 calories, 3.4 grams fat, 0.9 grams saturated fat, 0.9 grams polyunsaturated fat, 1.3 grams monounsaturated fat, 6 grams protein, 3 grams carbohydrate, 0.7 grams fiber, 31 mg cholesterol, 331 mg sodium, 204 mg potassium

* Chinese chili oil can be found in the Chinese grocery section of many stores or can be made by mixing together ⅓ cup peanut oil and 1½ tsp. hot red pepper flakes.

Chinese Chicken Salad
China

Servings: 6

I learned to make this salad in Cantonese cooking school in San Francisco's Chinatown. The recipe is written with guests in mind; you can easily cut it in half.

3 cups cooked boneless chicken (meat from one 3-4 lb. chicken;
   see **Chicken and Stock**, page 28)
6 to 8 green onions
¼ cup fresh cilantro, chopped
⅓ cup dry roasted peanuts, coarsely chopped
1 tbs. soy sauce
¼ cup chicken stock **or** ¼ cup water with ½ tsp. instant chicken bouillon
1 tbs. canola oil
2 tsp. sesame oil
½ tsp. dry mustard
1 tsp. fresh ginger root, peeled, minced
freshly ground pepper
1 lb. romaine lettuce (one medium head), crosscut into ¼" wide shreds

2 tbs. sesame seeds*, toasted
2 tomatoes, each cut into six wedges
fresh cilantro sprigs (optional)

Into a large bowl, shred chicken, pulling meat apart lengthwise into ¼" to ½" wide pieces. Crosscut green onions into 4 or 5 pieces and then lengthwise into thin slivers. Add onions, cilantro and peanuts to chicken and toss together. In a small bowl, mix together soy sauce, broth, oils, mustard and ginger. Pour dressing over chicken mixture, add pepper to taste and toss well. Arrange lettuce on a serving platter and top with dressed chicken mixture. Sprinkle toasted seeds on top. Arrange tomato wedges around edge of platter. Garnish with sprigs of cilantro if desired.

Nutritional information per serving   250 calories, 14.5 grams fat, 2.5 grams saturated fat, 4.5 grams polyunsaturated fat, 6.4 grams monounsaturated fat, 24 grams protein, 7 grams carbohydrate, 3.3 grams fiber, 58 mg cholesterol, 283 mg sodium, 568 mg potassium

*To Toast Seeds: seeds can be toasted in the oven, microwave, or skillet on top of the stove. Watch closely and stir periodically, especially once they start to brown; they can burn easily.

Chicken and Stock

4 cups

I usually double this recipe, squeezing two chickens into a 10" diameter pot. You get twice the results for the time invested.

1 (3-4 lbs.) fryer chicken
1½ quarts water
1 small onion, quartered
1 leek, halved lengthwise, washed
   cut into chunks (optional)
1 carrot, cut into chunks

1 stalk celery, cut into chunks
1 tsp. salt
3 sprigs parsley
¼ tsp. thyme
1 bay leaf

Wash chicken well; discard neck and innards. Place in a pot just large enough around to contain chicken. Add water. If water does not cover chicken, you can turn bird over when half cooked or add more water and extend the reduction time at the end. Bring water to a boil. Skim off any froth that forms. Add remaining ingredients and reduce heat so water just trembles. Cook, partially covered, for 45 minutes. Remove chicken. Allow pot to continue simmering, uncovered. When cool enough to handle, about 45 minutes, remove chicken meat (about 1 lb. or 3 cups) from bones, returning all skin and bones to simmering pot. Simmer an additional hour, uncovered, allowing liquid to reduce. Pour stock mixture through a colander, fine sieve or cheesecloth to strain. Discard bones and vegetables. Divide into 1- or 2-cup portions; chill; remove and discard all fat. Refrigerate, if used within five days, or freeze for extended storage. Makes about 4 cups. For richer stock, return strained broth to pan and boil until reduced to 3 cups.

Nutritional information per one cup serving of salted, canned chicken broth 39 calories, 1.4 grams fat, 0.4 grams saturated fat, 0.3 grams polyunsaturated fat, 0.6 grams monounsaturated fat, 5 grams protein, 1 gram carbohydrate, 0 grams fiber, 1 mg cholesterol, 776 mg sodium, 210 mg potassium

Skewered Chicken with Peanut Sauce (Sate Ayam)
Indonesia

Servings: 4

Sate makes a substantial appetizer or it can be served as a main course. Stir-fried veggies and steamed rice round out a delicious meal.

1 lb. boneless chicken breast **or** lean pork loin

Marinade:

3 tbs. soy sauce	2 tbs. water
1 tbs. white sugar	1 tbs. lemon juice
1 tbs. molasses	2 cloves garlic, minced

Trim all skin and fat from meat and cut into ¾" cubes. Mix together remaining ingredients for marinade. Add meat and marinate at least 30 minutes. Thread onto skewers (soak wooden ones in water for 30 minutes before using to prevent burning) and broil or barbecue until done (pork should lose pink color). Accompany with **Peanut Sauce,** page 33, served in individual saucers.

Nutritional information per serving with 3 tbs. Peanut Sauce   247 calories, 9.9 grams fat, 1.8 grams saturated fat, 2.9 grams polyunsaturated fat, 4.4 grams monounsaturated fat, 32 grams protein, 8 grams carbohydrate, 1.3 grams fiber, 65 mg cholesterol, 443 mg sodium, 479 mg potassium

Twice-baked Cookies (page 106), Skewered Chicken with Peanut Sauce (page 30) and Christmas Salad (page 112) ▶

Peanut Sauce

1⅓ cups

Indonesia

This dipping sauce traditionally accompanies Sate.

½ cup chicken stock (see **Chicken and Stock**, page 28)
¼ cup onion, finely chopped
1 fresh, hot green chili pepper, or to taste
2 cloves garlic, minced
1½ tsp. fresh ginger root, peeled, minced
1 tbs. soy sauce
2 tbs. brown sugar
2 tbs. fresh lemon juice
½ cup natural crunchy peanut butter
½ cup chicken stock, or as needed

In a small saucepan, simmer onion in stock. Add chili, garlic, ginger, soy sauce, sugar and lemon. Stir in peanut butter, blending well. Thin with chicken stock to desired consistency. Serve with skewered pork or chicken.

Nutritional information per 3 tbs. 119 calories, 8.5 grams fat, 1.4 grams saturated fat, 2.6 grams polyunsaturated fat, 4.1 grams monounsaturated fat, 6 grams protein, 7 grams carbohydrate, 1.3 grams fiber, 0 mg cholesterol, 293 mg sodium, 179 mg potassium

◀ **Spicy Thai Noodles (page 34)**

Asia **33**

Spicy Thai Noodles
Thailand

Servings: 4

Do not limit your pasta experiences to Italian specialties. Move on to Asia for new taste (and convenience!) thrills.

2 tbs. brown sugar
3 tbs. soy sauce
⅓ cup rice vinegar
2 tbs. lemon juice
2 tsp. sesame oil
2 cloves garlic, minced
½ tsp. hot red pepper flakes
8 ozs. very thin spaghetti **or** vermicelli
½ cup carrot (one carrot), shredded
1 cup green onion (3 green onions), chopped into 6 pieces crosswise,
   then slivered lengthwise **or** 3 tbs. lemon grass, white stem portion,
   chopped crosswise
1 fresh hot red or green chili pepper*, sliced lengthwise very thin
2 cups Chinese cabbage, shredded
4 ozs. small shrimp **or** lean, roasted beef, cooked, cut into thin strips

¼ cup fresh cilantro, chopped (optional)
2 tbs. roasted peanuts, chopped (optional)
2" lengths of green onion (optional)
cilantro sprigs (optional)

In a large bowl, mix sugar, soy sauce, vinegar, lemon, oil, garlic and pepper together. In a large pot cook noodles al dente (just enough to retain a somewhat firm texture) in boiling, salted water. Drain and rinse briefly. Add noodles to dressing in bowl and toss well. Lift seasoned noodles onto a warmed serving platter, leaving extra dressing in bowl. Keep noodles warm, covered, in a slow oven. Pour leftover dressing into a large skillet or wok. Stir-fry carrot, onion and pepper for 1 to 2 minutes. Add cabbage, shrimp and cilantro, if used. Stir-fry 2 to 3 minutes, allowing liquid to reduce somewhat. Add vegetable mixture to noodles and mix gently. Garnish with peanuts, onion ``brushes'' (2" lengths of green onion with one end cut lengthwise into thin shreds) and cilantro sprigs, if desired. Serve hot as a main course or room temperature as a salad.

Nutritional information per serving   321 calories, 3.6 grams fat, 0.5 grams saturated fat, 1.6 grams polyunsaturated fat, 1.1 grams monounsaturated fat, 16 grams protein, 57 grams carbohydrate, 3.5 grams fiber, 42 mg cholesterol, 838 mg sodium, 540 mg potassium

* see **To Handle Fresh Chilies**, page 17

Sweet and Sour Pork

China

Instead of coating the pork cubes with batter and deep-fat frying them, this pork remains "bald," but the flavors are all there!

1 lb. lean boneless pork, cut into ¾" cubes
1 tbs. peanut **or** canola oil
salt and pepper to taste
¼ cup green onion, chopped
1 clove garlic, minced
½ cup chicken stock (see **Chicken and Stock**, page 28) **or**
   ½ cup water plus ½ tsp. instant chicken-flavored bouillon
1 carrot, peeled, crosscut into four pieces and then
   lengthwise into ⅛" matchsticks
1 red bell pepper, cut into 1" squares
1 green bell pepper, cut into 1" squares
4 tbs. red wine vinegar
1 tbs. cornstarch
4 tbs. sugar

1 tsp. soy sauce
1 tbs. tomato catsup

Heat oil in a large skillet and sauté pork, turning constantly, until cooked and browned, about 5 minutes. Season to taste. Remove meat to a serving platter and keep warm. Add green onion, garlic and chicken stock and deglaze pan, scraping any browned bits off the bottom. Add carrot and peppers and cook briefly, turning frequently, about 4 minutes. In a small bowl, mix vinegar and cornstarch well; blend in sugar, soy sauce and catsup. Add seasoning mixture to hot vegetables and stir to thicken evenly. Add pork to skillet and toss to coat with sauce. Turn out onto warmed platter, surrounded by rice or thin noodles. Serve immediately.

Nutritional information per serving   264 calories, 13 grams fat, 3.8 grams saturated fat, 2 grams polyunsaturated fat, 6.2 grams monounsaturated fat, 22 grams protein, 14 grams carbohydrate, 0.9 grams fiber, 60 mg cholesterol, 192 mg sodium, 461 mg potassium

British Isles

British fare, though rather unremarkable, includes creative potato dishes and game stews.

Mashed Potatoes and Cabbage (Colcannon)

Ireland

Servings: 4

This humble dish offers comfort on a chilly evening as well as nutrients to spare.

1½ lbs. boiling potatoes (3 medium)
1 tbs. butter
3 tbs. green onion, chopped (about 2 onions)
2 cups green cabbage, finely shredded

½ tsp. salt
⅓ cup nonfat milk, warmed
2 tbs. fresh parsley, chopped
freshly ground pepper

Steam potatoes until cooked but not mushy. Peel. Melt butter in a large skillet or wok; stir-fry onion and cabbage until cabbage wilts. Add salt. Mash potatoes using a masher, ricer or mixer (if a mixer is used, take care not to overbeat). Mix in milk and parsley. Add cabbage mixture and mix lightly. Season to taste. Serve at once in a heated serving dish.

Nutritional information per serving 228 calories, 3.2 grams fat, 1.9 grams saturated fat, 0.2 grams polyunsaturated fat, 0.9 grams monounsaturated fat, 5 grams protein, 46 grams carbohydrate, N/A fiber, 8 mg cholesterol, 321 mg sodium, N/A potassium

Rabbit Stew
England

Servings: 4

Curl up with a favorite British novel while this cooks in the oven. The wonderful aroma will transport you to the English countryside and send your imagination soaring.

1 (3 lbs.) fresh rabbit, quartered **or** frozen, defrosted rabbit
½ cup dry red wine
1 tbs. canola oil
1 large onion, sliced
1 bay leaf, halved
½ tsp. rosemary, crumbled
½ tsp. salt
⅓ lb. bacon, diced
¼ cup flour
3 tbs. canola oil
¼ cup shallots, minced **or** ¼ cup onion, minced

5 carrots, peeled, cut into ½" slices
1½ cups chicken stock, preferably homemade (see **Chicken and Stock**, page 28)
2 bay leaves
1 tsp. thyme
1 tsp. salt
freshly ground pepper
2 tbs. flour
½ cup port
3 tbs. red currant jelly

Wash rabbit and pat dry with paper towelling. In a glass or nonreactive bowl, combine wine, oil, onion, bay, rosemary and salt. Add rabbit, coating well with marinade; cover and refrigerate for 6 hours or overnight, turning rabbit several times. In a large ovenproof pot or Dutch oven, cook bacon over moderate heat, stirring, until crisp and golden. Remove to paper towelling. Discard bacon fat. Remove rabbit from marinade, saving liquid but discarding onion and bay. Dry rabbit with paper towelling. Shake rabbit pieces with flour in a brown paper bag, coating well and shaking off any excess. Add 2 tbs. oil to pot and brown rabbit on all sides, watching that it does not burn. Remove rabbit. Add additional 1 tbs. oil and sauté shallot and carrot 2 to 3 minutes over medium heat, stirring constantly. Add stock, bay, thyme, salt and pepper and scrape browned particles from bottom of pan. Return rabbit and bacon to pot, cover and cook in 350° oven for 1 hour. Rabbit should feel tender when pricked with a sharp fork. In a small jar, shake flour with port; add to pot along with jelly, mixing evenly. Return covered pot to oven for 10 to 15 minutes. Serve hot, directly from Dutch oven if possible.

Nutritional information per serving 414 calories, 15.5 grams fat, 2.3 grams saturated fat, 3.7 grams polyunsaturated fat, 8.6 grams monounsaturated fat, 34 grams protein, 35 grams carbohydrate, 3.6 grams fiber, 74 mg cholesterol, 1354 mg sodium, 864 mg potassium

Individual Meat Pies (Cornish Pasties)

12 pasties

Wales

Miners would often make a meal of these substantial food packets. Fresh fruit might be added for a complete menu.

Pastry:
4 cups whole wheat flour, very finely ground **or** all purpose flour
1 tsp. salt
⅔ cup vegetable shortening
13 to 14 tbs. ice cold water

In a large bowl, blend flour, salt and shortening together with a pastry cutter or by rubbing with your fingers, until mixture resembles coarse meal. Add ⅔ of the water all at once and mix quickly, trying to get mixture to hold together in a ball. Add remaining water, one tablespoon at a time, mixing only until mixture holds together. Wrap in plastic wrap or plastic bag and refrigerate at least one hour.

Filling:
1 lb. extra lean ground beef
1 cup onion, chopped
½ cup turnip, diced (1 small turnip)
2 cups potatoes, diced (1 lb. boiling potatoes)
2 tsp. salt
¼ tsp. pepper
1 egg white **or** whole egg, lightly beaten for glaze

Preheat oven to 400°. In a large bowl, mix uncooked filling ingredients together except for egg. On a lightly floured board, roll out half of dough to ⅛" thickness. Using a saucer or small bowl as a guide, cut 6" circles. Place ⅓ to ½ cup filling off center of circle, fold over and seal, pressing edges together with tines of a fork. Brush the top of each pasty with egg. Place on a baking sheet. Repeat with remaining dough and filling, making 12 pasties total. Bake at 400° for 15 minutes. Reduce heat to 350° and bake for 30 additional minutes.

Nutritional information per pasty   354 calories, 16.2 grams fat, 4.3 grams saturated fat, 3.6 grams polyunsaturated fat, 6.9 grams monounsaturated fat, 19 grams protein, 39 grams carbohydrate, 5.3 grams fiber, 36 mg cholesterol, 565 mg sodium, 468 mg potassium

Oatcakes
Scotland

These breakfast "crackers" offer an alternative to hot oatmeal. Simple fare, yes, but satisfying and "good for you" in terms of serum cholesterol management.

1¼ cups rolled oats
¼ tsp. baking powder
¼ tsp. salt
1 tbs. sugar

1 tbs. butter
3 tbs. water
½ cup rolled oats

Preheat oven to 350°. Process 1¼ cups oats into flour in a food processor or blender. Add baking powder, salt and sugar and mix. Melt butter in water (about 35 seconds on high in a microwave) and add to mixture, blending only until it forms a sticky mass. Spread ¼ cup oats on a board and turn dough onto it. Scatter remaining ¼ cup oats on top of dough. Pat into an 8" or 9" circle, pressing oats into top and bottom surfaces. Place on an ungreased cookie sheet. Using a dull knife, cut into 8 wedges. Bake 15 to 20 minutes, until lightly browned on edges. Serve hot with honey or jam and **Yogurt Cheese**, page 46, if desired.

Nutritional information per wedge 87 calories, 2.6 grams fat, 1.1 grams saturated fat, 0.5 grams polyunsaturated fat, 0.8 grams monounsaturated fat, 3 grams protein, 13 grams carbohydrate, 1.1 grams fiber, 4 mg cholesterol, 90 mg sodium, 63 mg potassium

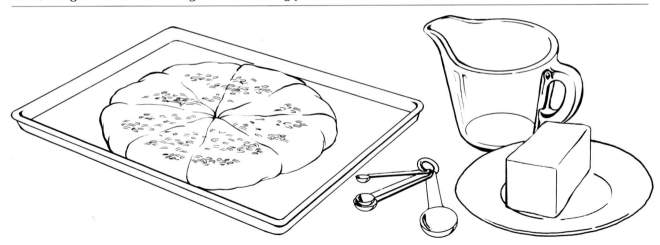

Yogurt Cheese

2 cups

This makes a nice spread, similar to cream cheese in texture. Use on breads, in dips or as a topping on desserts.

1 quart plain nonfat yogurt (use a natural yogurt rather
   than one with added thickener)

Place yogurt in a yogurt cheese funnel (or improvised version made by placing a filter paper in the top of a drip coffee maker). Place over a container to catch dripping whey. Let stand in refrigerator for 24 hours or until thickened to desired consistency. Discard whey. Use unflavored or add vanilla, fruits, herbs or other desired flavors. One quart of yogurt yields about 2 cups of yogurt cheese.

Nutritional information per cup 188 calories, 0 grams fat, 0 grams saturated fat, 0 grams polyunsaturated fat, 0.2 grams monounsaturated fat, 24 grams protein, 22 grams carbohydrate, 0 grams fiber, 3 mg cholesterol, 214 mg sodium, 762 mg potassium

Gingerbread

England

Servings: 9

Served plain or with yogurt, this makes a very satisfying breakfast cake or comforting dessert.

¼ cup canola oil
½ cup molasses
1 egg
¾ cup nonfat, plain yogurt

1 ⅔ cups whole wheat flour, very finely ground
1 tsp. baking soda
½ tsp. salt
1 tsp. ginger

Preheat oven to 350°. In a large mixer bowl, beat oil, molasses and egg together well. Add yogurt and mix well. Sift dry ingredients together. Add all at once to wet ingredients. Mix lightly; extra beating will toughen the cake. Turn batter into a nonstick 9" square pan. Bake 25 minutes or until center of cake springs back when touched lightly with fingertip. Cool briefly in pan on rack. Serve warm, with **Lemon Syrup**, page 48, if desired.

Nutritional information per serving 186 calories, 7.2 grams fat, 0.6 grams saturated fat, 2 grams polyunsaturated fat, 4.1 grams monounsaturated fat, 5 grams protein, 27 grams carbohydrate, 2.3 grams fiber, 31 mg cholesterol, 117 mg sodium, 303 mg potassium

Lemon Syrup

This is a delicious accompaniment to gingerbread as well as other desserts.

¾ cup sugar
1 cup water
zest (peel) of one large lemon*
¼ cup lemon juice (about 1 lemon)

Heat sugar, water and lemon zest in a small saucepan. Bring to boiling and continue to boil, uncovered, for 10 minutes. Remove from heat and add juice. Serve warm.

Nutritional information per 1⅓ tablespoon   67 calories, 0 grams fat, 0 grams protein, 17 grams carbohydrate, 0.1 grams fiber, 0 mg cholesterol, 1 mg sodium, 11 mg potassium

*Use a zester to peel long, very thin strips of the yellow portion of peel from lemon. If zester is not available, peel zest from lemon using vegetable peeler. Cut into very thin strips.

Oatcakes (page 44) with Yogurt Cheese (page 46) ▶

Central Europe

Recipes in this section reflect foods of Austria, Belgium, Germany, Hungary and Switzerland.

Oat Apple Cereal (Muesli)
Switzerland

Servings: 2

Muesli is the result of an attempt by a Swiss health spa to create the perfect food. The addition of oat bran makes an already super-nutritious dish even more so.

¼ cup oat bran
⅓ cup rolled oats
½ cup nonfat milk
1 tbs. dried fruit, chopped (raisins, currants, prunes, apricot, etc.)
1 tbs. honey
1 medium apple, cored, grated
1 tbs. fresh lemon juice
dash of cinnamon sugar (optional)

Mix bran, oats, milk, dried fruit and honey together. Cover and let stand overnight in refrigerator. Just before serving, add apple and lemon. Mix well.

Nutritional information per serving 201 calories, 2 grams fat, 0.3 grams saturated fat, 0.4 grams polyunsaturated fat, 0.3 grams monounsaturated fat, 7 grams protein, 41 grams carbohydrate, 4.7 grams fiber, 1 mg cholesterol, 33 mg sodium, 336 mg potassium

Marinated Brussels Sprouts

Belgium

Use a fruity, extra virgin olive oil and fresh tarragon, if available, for best flavors. These make a tasty, fiber-rich hors d'oeuvre or salad.

1 lb. fresh Brussels sprouts (about 20),
   washed and trimmed **or**
   1 (10 ozs.) pkg., frozen
1 tbs. olive oil
2 tbs. white wine vinegar
2 tbs. fresh lemon juice
1 clove garlic, minced

1 green onion, minced
1 tsp. tarragon
1 tsp. sugar
½ tsp. salt
freshly ground pepper
1 tbs. capers, drained (optional)

Steam Brussels sprouts over boiling water until tender but not overcooked, about 10 to 12 minutes. Cut Brussels sprouts in half lengthwise, if desired, after cooking. In a small bowl, whisk remaining ingredients together. Pour over hot vegetables. Marinate, refrigerated, for several hours or overnight for fullest flavor. Serve on fresh greens as a salad or with picks as an appetizer. About 5 Brussels sprouts make a serving.

Nutritional information per serving 88 calories, 3.8 grams fat, 0.5 grams saturated fat, 0.5 grams polyunsaturated fat, 2.5 grams monounsaturated fat, 4 grams protein, 13 grams carbohydrate, 4.4 grams fiber, 0 mg cholesterol, 295 mg sodium, 475 mg potassium

Sweet and Sour Cabbage (Rotkohl)
Germany

Servings: 7

*Serve this with **Sauerbraten**, page 58, potato pancakes and applesauce, and you have a classic German meal!*

1 tbs. canola oil
½ cup finely sliced onion
½ cup red wine vinegar
2 tbs. sugar
1 tsp. salt
1 bay leaf
1 small head red cabbage (about 2½ lbs.)
2 large tart apples, Granny Smith or Pippin, quartered, cored, thinly sliced
2 cups boiling water
freshly ground pepper
a splash or two of dry red wine **or** juice of half a lemon (optional)
1 to 2 tbs. red currant jelly (optional)
1 tsp. caraway seeds (optional)

In a large covered saucepan or soup pot, heat oil and sauté onion until soft. Mix in vinegar, sugar, salt and bay leaf. Discard outer leaf from cabbage and cut head into quarters. Remove core; thinly slice cabbage. Add, together with apple, to onion and seasonings in pot. Pour in boiling water, bring to a boil, cover and reduce to simmer. Cook 1½ hours, stirring occasionally, until most liquid is evaporated and cabbage is tender. Remove cover during last 20 minutes or so to accelerate evaporation. (Cabbage can be cooked in a microwave: omit water; cook about 20 minutes on high.) Remove bay leaf; season to taste. Add the wine or lemon and jelly, if desired, as a finishing touch. Caraway seeds are also favored by some. Serve hot.

Nutritional information per 1-cup serving   115 calories, 2.6 grams fat, 0.2 grams saturated fat, 0.8 grams polyunsaturated fat, 1.3 grams monounsaturated fat, 3 grams protein, 24 grams carbohydrate, 6 grams fiber, 0 mg cholesterol, 324 mg sodium, 433 mg potassium

Viennese Scalloped Veal (Wiener Schnitzel)
Austria

This delicious favorite satisfies our general guidelines of less than 15 grams of fat per serving. Choose lowfat accompaniments for the rest of your meal, and enjoy it all in good health!

½ lb. boneless veal, thinly sliced (¼") from leg or loin **or** turkey breast slices
1 egg
1 tbs. water

3 tbs. flour
6 tbs. fine, dry bread crumbs
4 tsp. canola oil
1 lemon, quartered into wedges, seeded
parsley sprigs (optional)

Using the side of a wooden mallet or cleaver, pound the slices of veal until they are very thin but not torn. A slice, originally ¼" thick, will enlarge two to three times. Beat egg with water. Place flour, egg-water mixture and crumbs into three separate shallow dishes or pie plates. Dip each slice of veal into flour, shaking off excess, into egg, and then into crumbs. Place on waxed paper. Using two large skillets, if possible (if not, do two batches), heat 2 tsp. of oil in each skillet. Cook the veal quickly, about 1 to 2 minutes per side, until lightly golden. Serve immediately with lemon, garnished with parsley if desired.

Nutritional information per serving 245 calories, 12.8 grams fat, 3.6 grams saturated fat, 2 grams polyunsaturated fat, 6.3 grams monounsaturated fat, 19 grams protein, 13 grams carbohydrate, 0.6 grams fiber, 142 mg cholesterol, 124 mg sodium, 227 mg potassium

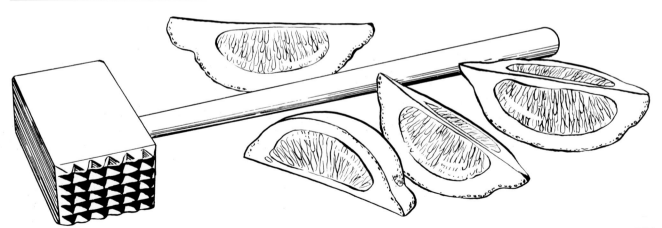

German Pot Roast (Sauerbraten)
Germany

Servings: 8

Hearty and relatively heart-healthy for a meat dish. Braising or stewing meats allows the skimming and removal of separated fat.

3 lbs. rump roast, trimmed of all fat

Marinade:

1 cup water
⅔ cup wine **or** cider vinegar
¼ cup onion, chopped
2 bay leaves

1 tsp. peppercorns, crushed*
1 tbs. paprika
4 whole cloves
½ tsp. thyme

Seasoning:

½ cup carrot, sliced or chopped
½ cup celery, chopped
½ cup onion, chopped
1 tsp. salt

2 cups water
8 gingersnap cookies (2")
⅓ cup raisins (optional)

Place meat in a glass or plastic container snug enough to surround at least ⅔ of roast with marinade. Heat marinade ingredients to hot but not boiling. Pour over meat. Cover and refrigerate one to two days, turning meat in marinade several times daily. To cook, remove roast from marinade and dry with paper towelling. Reserve marinade. Place roast fat side down in a Dutch oven or large cooking pot. Heat meat on all sides, using moderate heat, moving roast across bottom of pan and taking care not to burn meat. Add vegetables to pan and continue stirring several minutes. Remove bay leaves from marinade and discard. Add marinade to pot, along with salt and water. Heat to boiling, cover, reduce heat to simmer and cook, turning meat occasionally, for 3 hours. When tender, remove meat to a serving platter, keeping it warm. Skim all grease from cooking liquid and discard. Add gingersnaps, mashing them into liquid. Run gravy through a food mill or food processor to puree. Return to pan to reheat; add raisins, if desired. Slice roast across the grain and arrange on platter, surrounded by gravy. Pass extra gravy separately.

Nutritional information per serving   351 calories, 12.8 grams fat, 4.4 grams saturated fat, 0.9 grams polyunsaturated fat, 5.6 grams monounsaturated fat, 52 grams protein, 8 grams carbohydrate, 1.1 grams fiber, 126 mg cholesterol, 437 mg sodium, 1088 mg potassium

*To Crush Peppercorns: wrap peppercorns in several layers of plastic or waxed paper. Hit sharply with the broad side of a cleaver or wide knife until crushed.

Christmas Bread (Stollen)
Austria

16 slices

Although traditionally made with yeast and white flour, this bread now becomes more convenient as well as more nutritious.

¾ cup sugar
½ cup butter
1 cup lowfat cottage cheese
1 egg
1 tsp. vanilla
2 tbs. rum
¾ cup toasted almonds*, ground
2½ cups whole wheat flour,
  very finely ground

2 tsp. baking powder
½ tsp. salt
½ tsp. cardamom
½ cup currants
½ cup golden raisins
⅓ cup candied fruit **or**
  candied lemon peel
2 tbs. butter, melted
2 tbs. white sugar

Preheat oven to 350°. In a mixer bowl, cream sugar and butter together. Add cottage cheese, egg, vanilla, rum and almonds and mix well. Sift together flour, baking powder, salt and cardamom. Add to dough and mix well. Add dried and candied fruits and blend in. On a lightly floured board, roll or pat out dough into a 9" x 12" oval. Lightly crease oval lengthwise, a bit off center. Fold shorter portion on top of larger portion, taking care to mend any tears where it folds. Place a large brown bag, folded flat, on top of a large cookie sheet, unprinted side up. Carefully lift stollen onto paper-covered baking sheet. Bake 50 to 55 minutes; watch to prevent over-browning. Leave stollen on paper and slide from cookie sheet to rack to cool. Brush top with melted butter and sprinkle with sugar. Remove from paper when thoroughly cooled.

Nutritional information per serving   255 calories, 10.5 grams fat, 4.6 grams saturated fat, 1.1 grams polyunsaturated fat, 4.1 grams monounsaturated fat, 7 grams protein, 37 grams carbohydrate, 3.2 grams fiber, 35 mg cholesterol, 238 mg sodium, 215 mg potassium

*see **To Toast Nuts**, page 19

Spiced Honey Bars (Lebkuchen)

Germany

These cookie bars store particularly well.

2 eggs
½ cup sugar
1 cup honey
½ cup nonfat milk
¼ cup candied fruit, finely diced
1 tsp. grated lemon peel
½ cup toasted almonds*, ground
2 ¼ cups whole wheat flour,
   very finely ground

½ tsp. soda
¼ tsp. cloves
1½ tsp. cinnamon
1 tsp. nutmeg
½ tsp. allspice
¾ cup powdered sugar
1 tbs. fresh lemon juice
1-2 tbs. water

Preheat oven to 400°. In a mixer bowl, beat eggs and sugar until lemon-colored. Add honey and beat well. Add milk, fruit, peel and almonds and mix well. Sift flour, soda and spices together. Add to wet mixture and blend only until well-mixed. Turn into a greased and lightly floured 10" x 15" jelly-roll pan and spread out evenly. Bake 12 to 15 minutes or until cake rebounds when pressed lightly in the center. Cool in pan on a rack. Mix sugar, lemon and water for glaze; spread on cake while still slightly warm. When cool, cut into 1½" x 2½" bars. Store in a tin with a tight-fitting lid.

Nutritional information per bar 85 calories, 1.3 grams fat, 0.2 grams saturated fat, 0.3 grams polyunsaturated fat, 0.7 grams monounsaturated fat, 2 grams protein, 18 grams carbohydrate, 0.9 grams fiber, 14 mg cholesterol, 20 mg sodium, 53 mg potassium

*see **To Toast Nuts**, page 19

Mini Dumplings (Spaetzle)

Servings: 4

Hungary

These tiny dumplings replace noodles or rice as an accompaniment to **Sauerbraten**, *page 58, or* **Beef Stroganov**, *page 76.*

1½ cups all-purpose flour
½ tsp. salt
⅛ tsp. nutmeg
2 eggs

½ cup nonfat milk
3 quarts water
2 tsp. salt
buttered breadcrumbs (optional)

Sift dry ingredients into a mixing bowl. Add eggs and mix. Add milk slowly, mixing until smooth. In a large pan, bring salted water to a boil. Using a spaetzle maker (or substitute something with 3/16" diameter holes, such as a colander or potato ricer), press dough through holes directly into the boiling water. Dumplings need to cook 6 to 8 minutes; taste to be sure they are tender. Drain in a sieve or colander; serve immediately. Traditionally they are topped with buttered breadcrumbs. You can save the extra fat by dressing them up with gravy from accompanying dishes.

Nutritional information per serving   221 calories, 3.3 grams fat, 0.9 grams saturated fat, 0.6 grams polyunsaturated fat, 1.2 grams monounsaturated fat, 9 grams protein, 37 grams carbohydrate, 1.3 grams fiber, 138 mg cholesterol, N/A sodium, 128 mg potassium

Northern Europe

This chapter includes foods from Scandinavian countries, Holland, Poland and the Soviet Union.

Puffy Pancake (Dutch Baby)
Holland

Servings: 2

Serve this fast before the puff in the pancake goes poof.

2 eggs
½ cup nonfat milk
¼ tsp. salt
½ cup all-purpose flour

Grease a 9" pie plate or oven-proof skillet. Have all ingredients and oven cold. Blend eggs, milk, oil and salt well in a food processor or mixer. Add flour and mix well. (A few small lumps will not matter.) Pour into a pan. Turn oven to 425° and place pancake in cold oven. Bake for 20 minutes. Serve immediately. Pass lemon wedges and powdered sugar for topping. Sliced fruit also makes a nice topping.

Nutritional information per serving   214 calories, 6 grams fat, 1.8 grams saturated fat, 0.9 grams polyunsaturated fat, 2.3 grams monounsaturated fat, 11 grams protein, 27 grams carbohydrate, 0.9 grams fiber, 275 mg cholesterol, 368 mg sodium, 196 mg potassium

Summer's Here Vegetable Soup (page 72) ▶

Swedish Rye Bread (Limpa)
Sweden

2 loaves, 16 slices each

Rye grows better than wheat in the Northern European climate. Here rye and whole wheat flours combine for a satisfying "peasant bread."

1 tbs. active dry yeast
1 tsp. sugar
1 cup water (105°-115°)
¼ cup canola oil
¼ cup molasses
¼ cup sugar

1 tsp. fennel seed, crushed **or** anise seed
2 tbs. grated orange peel
2 tsp. salt
1⅓ cups water
2½ cups rye flour
3¾ cups whole wheat flour, very finely ground

Proof yeast by mixing it in sweetened warm water. In a large mixer bowl, blend together oil, molasses, sugar, fennel, orange peel, salt and water. Mix in yeast, when it begins to foam; add flours. Knead 5 to 7 minutes using a dough hook. Turn into a greased bowl and cover with plastic wrap. Allow to rise 1¼ hours. Punch down and let rest briefly. Divide dough in half. Shape each half into a round "peasant" or free-form loaf. Place on a nonstick baking sheet, cover, and allow to rise 45 minutes. Preheat oven to 350°; bake 40 minutes.

Nutritional information per slice   106 calories, 2.2 grams fat, 0.2 grams saturated fat, 0.7 grams polyunsaturated fat, 1.1 grams monounsaturated fat, 3 grams protein, 20 grams carbohydrate, 2.3 grams fiber, 0 mg cholesterol, 134 mg sodium, 105 mg potassium

◄ **Scallops in Wine Sauce (page 86)**

Poor Man's Caviar

Russia

3½ cups

This is a popular starter at a local Russian restaurant. I find it also makes an interesting sandwich filling.

1½ lb. eggplant (one large)
3 green bell peppers
1 tbs. canola oil
1 cup onion, finely chopped
  (one large onion)
2 cloves garlic, minced

1½ cups tomatoes, peeled, chopped
  (2 large tomatoes)
1 tsp. salt
freshly ground pepper
2 tbs. fresh lemon juice

Place untrimmed eggplant and peppers on a baking sheet and bake at 400°. Remove peppers after 30 minutes; cool on rack, covered with a dish towel. Continue cooking eggplant for 30 minutes more (one hour, total). Meanwhile, sauté onion and garlic in oil in a large skillet until cooked but not browned. Add tomatoes, salt and pepper. Cook uncovered, allowing extra liquid to evaporate. Remove skins, stems and seeds from peppers. Carefully remove eggplant from oven when cooked and pierce skin, allowing steam to escape.

Remove peel and stem from eggplant. Dice peppers and eggplant and add to tomato mixture in skillet. Add lemon. Simmer mixture for 15 minutes, uncovered, to reduce unnecessary liquid and blend flavors. Serve warm or chilled as a relish or appetizer with crispbread or pumpernickel.

__Nutritional information per ¼ cup__ 35 calories, 1.2 grams fat, 0.1 grams saturated fat, 0.4 grams polyunsaturated fat, 0.6 grams monounsaturated fat, 1 gram protein, 6 grams carbohydrate, 2.3 grams fiber, 0 mg cholesterol, 197 mg sodium, 216 mg potassium

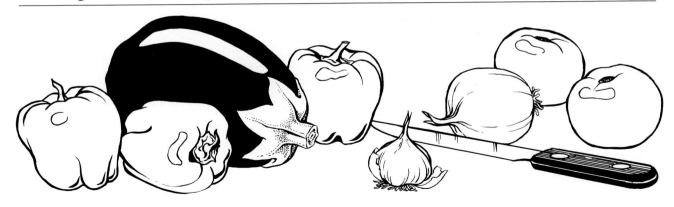

Summer's Here Vegetable Soup

Finland

The Finns celebrate the first warm, sunny days of summer with joy and feasting. This soup comprises the new vegetables of the season. Use the youngest, freshest vegetables you can find.

1½ cups carrots, peeled, sliced into thin rounds (4 small)
¾ cup fresh green peas (from 30 pods)
1 cup cauliflower broken into ½" flowerettes (1 very small head or partial head)
1½ cups small new red potatoes, skin on, cut into ½" cubes (4 small potatoes)
½ lb. green beans, ends trimmed, crosscut into ½" pieces
4 cups water
1 tsp. salt
2 cups fresh spinach, stemmed, finely chopped (½ bunch)
1 cup nonfat milk
3 tbs. all-purpose flour
½ cup nonfat instant dry milk powder
1 tbs. butter (optional)
½ lb. fresh shrimp, raw in shells (optional)
fresh dill

Wash and prepare vegetables and place them, except for the spinach, into a large pot. Add water and salt. Bring to a boil and cook for 5 minutes. Add spinach and cook for 5 minutes more. Place milk in a gravy shaker or jar with lid. Add flour, cover and shake vigorously. Add milk powder and shake again to mix completely. Stirring, add milk-flour mixture to soup pot. Continuing to stir, bring to a boil and cook only until soup thickens slightly, no more than two minutes.

If feeling very euphoric and sunstruck, garnish soup with shrimp. In a medium skillet, sauté shrimp in butter just until they turn pink. Rinse under cold water to stop cooking and cool enough to allow peeling and the removal of tails. Add to soup pot to heat. Serve garnished with fresh dill.

Nutritional information per 1-cup serving   130 calories, 0.4 grams fat, 0.1 grams saturated fat, 0.2 grams polyunsaturated fat, 0 grams monounsaturated fat, 7 grams protein, 26 grams carbohydrate, 5.2 grams fiber, 1 mg cholesterol, 384 mg sodium, 689 mg potassium

Stuffed Cabbage Rolls
Poland

Definitely an olde world favorite: simple and satisfying.

3 lbs. green cabbage (one large head)
½ cup uncooked brown rice **or** converted white rice
1 cup water **or** beef broth
1 tsp. salt
¼ tsp. pepper
¼ tsp. allspice
1 tbs. canola oil
1 cup onion, chopped
¾ lb. ground turkey **or** extra lean ground beef
1 egg, lightly beaten
1 (15 ozs.) can tomato sauce
1 (28 ozs.) can whole, peeled tomatoes, broken apart
1 tsp. dill
½ tsp. salt
freshly ground pepper
plain nonfat yogurt (optional)

Remove core from head of cabbage. Place head in a large casserole dish, core end down, and cover half way with water. Cover dish tightly with plastic wrap. Microwave on high for 10 minutes (or cook in boiling water or over steam in a large pot). Carefully remove head and separate leaves, one by one. Cut away tough central rib, about 2", from each leaf. Return any leaves that are not completely softened to the hot water and microwave on high, covered, 5 minutes longer. To cook rice: bring water to a boil in a medium saucepan. Add salt, pepper, allspice and rice; cover tightly; simmer for 45 minutes (or 20 if converted rice is used) or until liquid is all absorbed. In a large skillet, heat oil and sauté onion until soft. Remove from heat. Reserve a small amount of cooked onion in a large bowl for the sauce. To remaining onion, add turkey and rice and mix well. Stir in egg. To reserved onion in bowl, add tomato sauce, tomatoes and remaining seasonings to make sauce. Pour a small amount of sauce into a large baking dish (9" x 13") to cover the bottom. To make cabbage rolls, place ¼ cup of meat-rice mixture (or less for smaller leaves) on leaf at core end. Roll up once, turn in sides, and continue rolling to rounded edge. Place rolls seam side down, side by side, in a baking dish. Cover completely with sauce. Bake, uncovered, in a 350° oven for 1 hour. Serve with plain yogurt on top or on the side, if desired.

Nutritional information per roll 139 calories, 5.1 grams fat, 1.4 grams saturated fat, 1.3 grams polyunsaturated fat, 2.2 grams monounsaturated fat, 10 grams protein, 16 grams carbohydrate, 3.3 grams fiber, 40 mg cholesterol, 555 mg sodium, 573 mg potassium

Beef with Mushrooms in Cream Sauce (Beef Stroganov)
Russia

Servings:4

Created in Russia for a count, this dish has attained world-wide popularity.

1 tbs. canola oil
2 cups onions, thinly sliced
½ lb. fresh mushrooms, sliced
½ tbs. canola oil
1 lb. boneless beef sirloin, all fat removed, sliced very thinly
2 tsp. powdered mustard
1 tsp. sugar
1 tsp. salt
2 tbs. water
freshly ground pepper
1 cup nonfat plain yogurt, room temperature

In a large sauté pan, heat oil and sauté onions until soft. Add mushrooms and cook an additional 5 minutes, stirring. Simmer, uncovered, until liquid is eliminated. Turn vegetables onto hot platter. Clean pan. In ½ tbs. oil, sauté meat over high heat until browned and liquid is evaporated. Mix mustard, sugar, salt and water together to form a thin paste. Return vegetables to pan with meat and stir in seasoning. Mix well. Remove from heat and stir in yogurt. Do not heat; some separation may occur, but it is normal. Serve immediately, accompanied with **Spaetzle**, page 64, noodles or rice.

Nutritional information per serving 362 calories, 15.3 grams fat, 4.5 grams saturated fat, 2.1 grams polyunsaturated fat, 7.9 grams monounsaturated fat, 40 grams protein, 14 grams carbohydrate, 2.6 grams fiber, 102 mg cholesterol, 721 mg sodium, 943 mg potassium

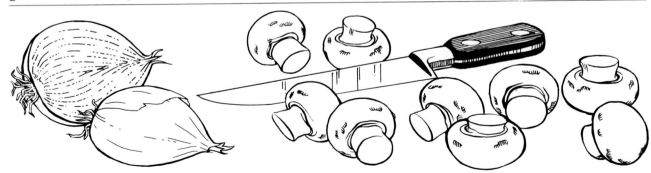

Strawberries Romanov
Russia

Servings: 4

Definitely a dessert for royalty!

4 cups fresh strawberries, halved **or** 1 lb. frozen, unsweetened strawberries **or**
2 cups raspberries
¼ cup kirsch or orange-flavored liqueur
1 cup lowfat vanilla **Yogurt Cheese**, page 46

Toss berries with 3 tbs. liqueur and chill for 30 to 60 minutes. Whisk yogurt with 1 tbs. liqueur. Serve berries in chilled dessert dishes, topped with yogurt.

Nutritional information per serving   167 calories, 1.6 grams fat, 0.6 grams saturated fat, 0.3 grams polyunsaturated fat, 0.4 grams monounsaturated fat, 5 grams protein, 36 grams carbohydrate, 3.4 grams fiber, 4 mg cholesterol, 33 mg sodium, 369 mg potassium

France

Ever since 1533, when Catherine de Medici took her Italian cooks to France, the French have eaten grand cuisine.

French Onion Soup
France

This popular soup is so easy to make you will find yourself looking for excuses to serve it to family and friends.

1 lb. onions, thinly sliced (about 2 onions)
1 tbs. olive oil
1 tbs. flour
4 cups beef stock **or** 4 cups water plus 4 tsp. beef-flavored instant bouillon
4 slices French bread, each 1" thick
2 tsp. olive oil (optional)
1 clove garlic, cut in half lengthwise (optional)
4 ozs. Swiss cheese, grated
salt and pepper to taste

In a large, heavy-bottomed saucepan, heat oil, add onions and cook over moderate heat, stirring occasionally until soft and golden brown, about 20 to 30 minutes. Sprinkle flour over onions and cook for several minutes, stirring. Heat stock and add to onions, stirring well. Season to taste. Place bread on a baking sheet and toast on both sides in a 350° oven. If desired, brush slices with oil and rub with cut clove of garlic prior to toasting. Top each toasted bread slice with ¼ of the cheese. Return to the oven and heat until cheese is melted but not rubbery. Serve soup with hot cheesy toast on top. **Or** ladle soup into overproof bowls, top each with toasted bread, add cheese and bake in a 350° oven until cheese melts. Run under hot broiler to brown, if desired.

Nutritional information per serving   300 calories, 13.5 grams fat, 6.2 grams saturated fat, 1.2 grams polyunsaturated fat, 5.3 grams monounsaturated fat, 16 grams protein, 29 grams carbohydrate, 2.4 grams fiber, 27 mg cholesterol, 1062 mg sodium, 371 mg potassium

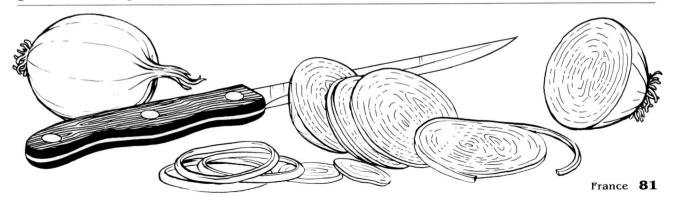

Tuna Vegetable Salad (Salad Nicoise)

Servings: 4

France

This popular salad originated in Nice on the Mediterranean coast of France where seafood is abundant.

1 large head butter **or** looseleaf lettuce, torn into large bite-sized pieces
4 small new potatoes, preferably red, steamed, unpeeled
4 fresh tomatoes, quartered
2 hard-boiled eggs, peeled, quartered
2 cups green beans, cooked, cut into 2" lengths
8 ripe olives, pitted
1 (6½ ozs.) can white albacore tuna, packed in water, drained
8 anchovy fillets, drained
1 recipe **French Vinaigrette**, page 83
¼ cup fresh parsley, chopped

Arrange the lettuce on four large plates. Artistically arrange ¼ of the potatoes, tomatoes, eggs, beans, olives, tuna and anchovies on each plate. Drizzle ¼ of the salad dressing over each salad. Sprinkle parsley on top.

Nutritional information per serving   420 calories, 17.3 grams fat, 3.1 grams saturated fat, 2.3 grams polyunsaturated fat, 10.4 grams monounsaturated fat, 28 grams protein, 42 grams carbohydrate, 8 grams fiber, 173 mg cholesterol, 527 mg sodium, 1317 mg potassium

Oil and Vinegar Salad Dressing (Vinaigrette)

France

Use this on any assortment of salad greens and veggies.

3 tbs. extra virgin olive oil
2 tbs. white wine vinegar
2 tbs. fresh lemon juice
¼ tsp. dry mustard
¼ tsp. salt
freshly ground pepper

Whisk ingredients together in a small bowl. Remix just before using.

Nutritional information per serving   93 calories, 10.2 grams fat, 1.4 grams saturated fat, 0.9 grams polyunsaturated fat, 7.5 grams monounsaturated fat, 0 grams protein, 1 gram carbohydrate, 0 grams fiber, 0 mg cholesterol, 144 mg sodium, 18 mg potassium

Asparagus with Hollandaise
France

Servings: 4

For a French feast, start with **French Onion Soup***, page 80, serve* **Asparagus with Hollandaise***,* **Scallops in Wine Sauce***, page 88, and steamed rice, and conclude with* **Poached Pears***, page 90. C'est magnifique!*

1 lb. fresh asparagus, white ends snapped off

Steam or boil asparagus, five to ten minutes, until just tender when a sharp fork easily pierces broken end of stem. Serve hot with **Mock Hollandaise**, page 87.

Nutritional information per serving with ¼ cup sauce 70 calories, 1.7 grams fat, 0.5 grams saturated fat, 0.3 grams polyunsaturated fat, 0.6 grams monounsaturated fat, 7 grams protein, 9 grams carbohydrate, 1.8 grams fiber, 69 mg cholesterol, 309 mg sodium, 440 mg potassium

---

Mock Hollandaise Sauce

France

1 cup

Broccoli, cauliflower and poached salmon are but a few of the foods that enjoy getting dressed up in this light, lemony sauce.

½ cup water
1 tbs. cornstarch
¼ cup nonfat instant dry milk
1 egg, beaten

2 tbs. fresh lemon juice
½ tsp. salt
freshly ground pepper

Shake or blend cornstarch with water. In a small saucepan, mix cornstarch mixture with milk powder, egg, lemon juice, salt and pepper. Whisk over medium heat until thickened. Watch carefully as this occurs suddenly. Whisk briskly as sauce thickens; remove from heat immediately and continue whisking for 1 to 2 minutes. Sauce will be light and fluffy.

Nutritional information per ¼-cup serving 44 calories, 1.5 grams fat, 0.4 grams saturated fat, 0.2 grams polyunsaturated fat, 0.6 grams monounsaturated fat, 3 grams protein, 5 grams carbohydrate, 0.1 grams fiber, 69 mg cholesterol, 307 mg sodium, 440 mg potassium

Scallops in Wine Sauce (Coquilles Saint-Jacques)
France

Servings: 4

If you have seashell dishes, use them to serve this elegant dish. Although the recipe suggests four main course servings, you can stretch this to six or eight portions if you make it a fish course or starter.

1 cup chicken stock, preferably homemade (see **Chicken and Stock**, page 28) **or** 1 cup plus 1 tsp. chicken-flavored instant bouillon
1 cup dry white wine
¼ cup shallots, minced **or** ¼ cup scallions, chopped
1 stalk celery, chopped
1 small bay leaf
¼ tsp. salt
5 whole peppercorns
¾ lb. scallops
⅓ lb. fresh mushrooms, sliced into ``umbrellas''
2 tbs. butter
3 tbs. flour
1 cup nonfat milk with ⅓ cup instant nonfat dry milk powder
   or 1 cup evaporated skim milk

1 tbs. fresh lemon juice
salt and pepper to taste
¼ cup dry, fine bread crumbs
2 tbs. Parmesan cheese, grated
2 tbs. fresh parsley, finely chopped

In a medium saucepan, mix stock, wine, shallot, celery, bay leaf, salt and peppercorns. Bring to a boil, reduce heat, and simmer, uncovered, for 20 minutes. Strain through a sieve into a 10" or 12" saucepan or skillet; discard celery mixture and set aside empty saucepan. Add scallops and mushrooms to liquid and cook over moderate heat for 5 minutes. Remove scallops and mushrooms to a sieve held over pan. When drained, set aside. Raise heat to high and reduce liquid to one cup. In original medium saucepan, melt butter. Add flour and whisk over medium heat for two minutes until bubbly but not browned. Remove from heat; add reduced liquid, whisking constantly to prevent lumping. Add milk; mix well. Mix in lemon juice. Adjust seasoning. Add scallops and mushrooms to sauce. Divide among 4 serving shells or turn into a shallow 1-quart casserole. Mix crumbs, cheese and parsley together and sprinkle on top. Heat until bubbly in a 375° oven, about 10 minutes, browning crumbs lightly under the broiler, if desired.

Nutritional information per serving   282 calories, 8.9 grams fat, 4.8 grams saturated fat, 0.9 grams polyunsaturated fat, 2.4 grams monounsaturated fat, 28 grams protein, 22 grams carbohydrate, 1.8 grams fiber, 65 mg cholesterol, 770 mg sodium, 927 mg potassium

Poached Pears
France

Servings: 4

*The flavor of this dessert will be most elegant when a quality wine is used. Serve with **Biscotti**, page 106, to soak up any extra syrup.*

2 tbs. lemon juice
1 tsp. grated lemon peel
1½ cups red wine
¼ cup sugar
1 3" stick of cinnamon, broken in half **or** ½ tsp. cinnamon
1½ lb. (4 small) firm but ripe pears
fresh mint sprigs (optional)

Mix lemon, peel, wine, sugar and cinnamon together in a saucepan large enough to hold pear halves in one layer. Cut pears in half lengthwise and remove core. Peel pears; place each peeled half directly in poaching liquid to prevent browning. Bring to a boil, cover, reduce heat and simmer about 15 minutes or until pears are tender but not mushy. Using a slotted spoon, remove pears to serving or storage plate. Continue cooking syrup over

88   France

moderately high heat, about 5 to 10 minutes, until reduced to a thicker syrup. Remove cinnamon stick and pour syrup over pears. Serve warm or chilled. Garnish with a sprig of fresh mint if desired.

Nutritional information per serving   126 calories, 0.4 grams fat, 0 grams saturated fat, 0.1 grams polyunsaturated fat, 0.1 grams monounsaturated fat, 1 gram protein, 30 grams carbohydrate, 3 grams fiber, 0 mg cholesterol, 5 mg sodium, 235 mg potassium

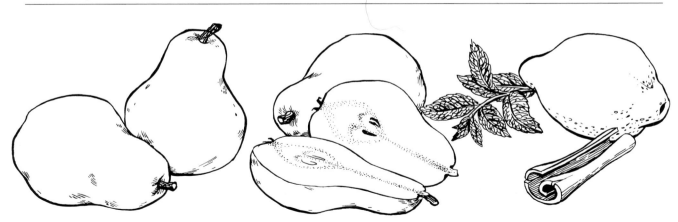

Italy

Italians are a food-loving people. It's no wonder. Pasta, pesto, polenta, panettone . . . the whole world can love this food!

Layered Pasta Casserole (Lasagna)
Italy

Servings: 15

Take your choice of "red-white-green" (vegetarian) or traditional (meat) versions. Either way, the recipe is super-fast, cooking the pasta in the casserole as it bakes.

Cheese layers:
1 egg, beaten
16 ozs. part skim ricotta cheese
16 ozs. dry curd (nonfat) cottage cheese
4 ozs. part skim mozzarella cheese, grated
1 tsp. oregano
¼ cup fresh parsley, chopped **or** 1 tbs. dried parsley flakes

Vegetarian layers:
1 lb. fresh Swiss chard, destemmed, coarsely chopped, steamed
   or
1 lb. spinach, destemmed, chopped, steamed

Meat layers:
3 ozs. Italian sausage, casing removed, crumbled and browned in
   a small skillet, drained of fat

Tomato layer:
4 cups **Tomato Sauce,** page 110
   or
1 (32 ozs.) jar spaghetti or marinara sauce

⅔ cup fresh bread crumbs (2 slices bread)
⅓ cup Parmesan cheese, grated
1 (8 ozs.) can tomato sauce
8 ozs. wide lasagna noodles, uncooked

   Preheat oven to 350°. In a large bowl, combine ingredients for cheese layer.
Prepare remaining layers. In a small bowl, stir together bread crumbs and
Parmesan. To assemble lasagna: spread 8 ozs. tomato sauce on the bottom of
a 13" x 9" glass or nonreactive casserole dish. Arrange ⅓ of the uncooked

pasta on tomato sauce. Top with ½ cheese layer, ½ either meat or vegetarian layer, ⅓ tomato layer, ⅓ pasta, remaining cheese layer, remaining meat or vegetarian layer, ⅓ tomato layer, remaining pasta and remaining tomato layer, *covering the pasta completely.* Distribute Parmesan and crumbs evenly on top. Cover very tightly with foil. Since the pasta will cook during baking, it is essential to contain enough liquid in the casserole to allow for adequate softening of the noodles. Bake for 50 minutes. Remove foil and bake 10 minutes longer. Allow to stand for 15 to 20 minutes before serving.

Nutritional information per serving of vegetarian version   220 calories, 7.6 grams fat, 3.2 grams saturated fat, 1 gram polyunsaturated fat, 2.8 grams monounsaturated fat, 16 grams protein, 23 grams carbohydrate, 2 grams fiber, 35 mg cholesterol, 522 mg sodium, 513 mg potassium

Nutritional information per serving of meat version   232 calories, 9 grams fat, 3.7 grams saturated fat, 1.2 grams polyunsaturated fat, 3.4 grams monounsaturated fat, 17 grams protein, 22 grams carbohydrate, 1.4 grams fiber, 40 mg cholesterol, 510 mg sodium, 416 mg potassium

Bean and Noodle Soup (Pasta e Fagioli)   Servings: 11
Italy

You will know you have eaten real food after a bowl of this soup.

1⅓ cups dry white beans (Great Northern or navy) **or** cranberry beans **or**
   2 (15 ozs. each) cans white beans (cannellini)*
10 cups water
1 tsp. salt
7 cups water
2 tsp. instant beef-flavored bouillon (optional)
4 ozs. extra-lean ham, diced **or** hambone or hamhock
   (the latter will add more fat than the lean ham)
1 onion, chopped
1 carrot, peeled, chopped
1 celery stalk, sliced
2 cloves garlic, minced
1 bay leaf
1 lb. fresh tomatoes, chopped **or**
   1 (15 ozs.) can whole, peeled Italian tomatoes, juice included

2 tbs. parsley, chopped
6 ozs. (1½ cups) dry macaroni **or** other tubular pasta
salt and pepper to taste
Parmesan cheese, grated (optional)

Sort beans. Soak: cover beans with 10 cups water and 1 tsp. salt, bring to a boil, cook 2 minutes, remove from heat, cover and let stand for 1 to 4 hours. Drain. In a large pot, place drained beans with 7 cups of water, bouillon, ham, vegetables, garlic and bay leaf. (Do not add tomatoes until beans are tender.) Bring to a boil, reduce heat and simmer, partially covered, about 1½ hours, until beans are tender. Remove 1 cup of beans and puree **or** mash them against the side of the pan to create thickening. Remove bay leaf and bones, if used. Add tomatoes, parsley and pasta and cook 15 minutes longer. Serve garnished with Parmesan cheese, if desired.

Nutritional information per 1-cup serving   165 calories, 1.2 grams fat, 0.3 grams saturated fat, 0.4 grams polyunsaturated fat, 0.3 grams monounsaturated fat, 10 grams protein, 30 grams carbohydrate, 2.3 grams fiber, 5 mg cholesterol, 220 mg sodium, 486 mg potassium

*If canned beans are used, omit soaking instructions.   Place drained beans in large pot with 4 cups of cooking water and cook beans, vegetables and seasonings for 30 minutes before adding pasta.

Eggplant Parmesan
(Parmigiana di Melanzane)
Italy

Servings: 6

You will not want to go back to the greasy versions of this classic dish once you have eaten it this way.

1½ lbs. eggplant
salt
2 cups **Tomato Sauce**, page 110 **or** 2 cups bottled marinara
6 ozs. part skim mozzarella cheese, grated
2 tbs. Parmesan, grated

Trim ends from eggplant and slice into ½" rounds. Sprinkle both sides of each slice with salt and let stand for 2 minutes. Rinse salt off and pat dry with paper towels. Place slices in a single layer on a nonstick cookie sheet. Bake in 350° oven for 15 minutes. Turn slices over and bake another 15 minutes. Slices should be soft when touched with fingertip. Cook slightly longer if not tender. In the bottom of a nonstick 2-quart shallow ovenproof serving dish, spread ¼ cup Tomato Sauce. Layer half the eggplant, half the remaining

Tomato Sauce, half the mozzarella, repeat and top with Parmesan cheese. Bake, covered, at 350° for 25 minutes. Remove cover and continue baking 10 minutes more. Serve hot.

Nutritional information per serving   151 calories, 6.7 grams fat, 3.5 grams saturated fat, 0.4 grams polyunsaturated fat, 2.3 grams monounsaturated fat, 10 grams protein, 15 grams carbohydrate, 5 grams fiber, 18 mg cholesterol, N/A sodium, 581 mg potassium

Pizza
Italy

The Italians make pizza dough with white flour. This recipe offers an alternative approach, using whole wheat flour for added nutrition and fiber.

Dough:
1 tbs. dry active yeast
1 tsp. sugar
1¼ cups warm water (105°-115°)
1 tsp. salt
¼ cup olive oil
3¼ cups whole wheat flour, very finely ground **or** all-purpose flour

Pizza sauce:
1 (8 ozs.) tomato sauce
2 cloves garlic, minced
1 tsp. oregano
1 tsp. basil
¾ tsp. anise seed
¼ tsp. salt

Toppings (optional):
Italian sausage, precooked, crumbled, well-drained
salami, thinly sliced or diced
lean ham strips
bell pepper rounds or strips
mushroom slices
zucchini or eggplant rounds, thinly cut
Italian plum tomato slices
marinated artichoke hearts, drained, sliced
ripe olives, sliced
anchovy fillets, drained, whole or chopped

Cheese:
6 ozs. part skim mozzarella cheese, grated

Proof yeast in warm, sweetened water. When foamy, add to remaining dough ingredients in a large mixer bowl. Mix well; knead for 5 to 7 minutes. Cover dough with plastic wrap and let rise about one hour. Punch down. Dough can rise again, up to one hour, or be shaped immediately.

Twenty minutes before baking, preheat oven to 450°. Line middle shelf in oven with pizza tiles, if available. To shape pizza, divide dough into two parts. Working with one part at a time, on a lightly floured board, roll dough into a 10" circle. Finish shaping by hand: gently stretch center portion of circle, working dough into a thicker mass at the edges. The finished circle should be about 13" to 14" across. Place dough on a pizza screen or pizza pan with many holes or wooden pizza paddle dusted with coarse cornmeal if using hot tiles. Spread half of tomato sauce on dough, leaving outer edge unsauced. Add toppings, if desired, and sprinkle half of cheese on top. Place screen or pan in hot oven or slide pizza off paddle onto preheated tiles. Bake about 10 minutes, watching that cheese does not brown and become rubbery. Repeat for second pizza.

Nutritional information per slice without toppings 146 calories, 5.7 grams fat, 1.6 grams saturated fat, 0.6 grams polyunsaturated fat, 3 grams monounsaturated fat, 6 grams protein, 19 grams carbohydrate, 2.8 grams fiber, 6 mg cholesterol, 303 mg sodium, 166 mg potassium

Poached Pears (page 88) ▶

Basil Sauce (Pesto)
Italy

You can make pesto year round: use fresh basil in the summer; make the spinach/parsley/dried basil version when the fresh herb is not available.

2 cups (packed) fresh basil leaves, destemmed
or
2 cups (packed) fresh spinach leaves, destemmed **plus** ½ cup (packed) parsley leaves, destemmed **plus** 2 tbs. dried basil

¼ cup olive oil
2 cloves garlic
2 tbs. pine nuts **or** sunflower seeds
¼ cup Parmesan cheese, grated
½ tsp. salt

Puree all ingredients well in a food processor. To serve: toss with 1 lb. pasta (linguine, vermicelli, shells, etc.) cooked al dente (just enough to retain a somewhat firm texture) or use as cocktail spread on crispbread or with Italian breadsticks.

Nutritional information per 2 tbs. pesto   130 calories, 12.6 grams fat, 2.2 grams saturated fat, 1.8 grams polyunsaturated fat, 7.8 grams monounsaturated fat, 3 grams protein, 3 grams carbohydrate, 1.5 grams fiber, 3 mg cholesterol, 258 mg sodium, 218 mg potassium

Cheese-filled Turnover (Calzone)
Italy

2 calzone, 2 servings each

Calzone, like pizza, bakes best in a wood-burning oven. But do not let this stop you from making your own at home.

Dough:
2 tsp. dry active yeast
¾ cup warm water (105°-115°)
1 tsp. sugar
2 tbs. olive oil
½ tsp. salt
1¾ cups whole wheat flour, very finely ground
¼ cup rye flour **or** whole wheat flour, very finely ground

Filling:
6 ozs. part skim ricotta **or** goat cheese, crumbled
4 ozs. part skim mozzarella cheese, grated
2 ozs. extra-lean ham **or** prosciutto, diced
2 tbs. fresh parsley, minced
2 tbs. fresh chives, minced, **or** green onion

½ tsp. mixed Italian herbs (oregano, marjoram, basil, thyme) **or**
   2 tsp. minced fresh herbs
freshly ground pepper

   Proof yeast in warm, sweetened water. When foamy, add yeast to remaining ingredients in a large mixer bowl. Mix well; knead 5 to 7 minutes. Cover and let rise until doubled, about one hour. Punch down. You can let dough rise again until needed (no longer than 1 hour) or shape immediately.
   Twenty minutes before baking, line middle shelf in oven with pizza tiles, if available. Preheat oven to 450°. To make calzone: divide dough in half. On a lightly floured board, roll each portion of dough into a 10" circle. Mix filling ingredients together and place half of the cheese mixture on half of each circle of dough. Fold over the unfilled half, making a turnover. Moisten inside of edges lightly and seal well, rolling edge slightly and crimping decoratively. Brush surface with olive oil, if desired, and dust lightly with herbs. Place directly on hot pizza tiles or on a pizza screen and bake for 10 to 15 minutes, until golden brown.

Nutritional information per serving   417 calories, 16.7 grams fat, 6.3 grams saturated fat, 1.4 grams polyunsaturated fat, 7.7 grams monounsaturated fat, 23 grams protein, 47 grams carbohydrate, 6.2 grams fiber, 36 mg cholesterol, 658 mg sodium, 378 mg potassium

---

Twice-baked Cookies (Biscotti)
Italy

These cookie sticks are appearing in delis and eateries across the land. It is much less expensive to make your own, and you don't have to stop with one, that way.

2 cups whole, unsalted, unblanched
    almonds*, toasted
½ cup butter
1½ cups sugar
2 eggs
3 cups whole wheat flour,
    very finely ground

1 tsp. baking powder
½ tsp. salt
½ tsp. anise seeds, finely crushed
8 ozs. bittersweet **or**
    semisweet chocolate (optional)

Preheat oven to 325°. In a large mixer bowl, cream butter and sugar together. Add eggs and beat until smooth. Sift flour, baking powder and salt together. Chop almonds somewhat coarsely. Add sifted dry ingredients along with seeds and almonds to batter. Mix briefly until dough pulls together. Divide dough into three equal parts. On a greased cookie sheet, pat each third into a strip

3" x 8", about 1" high. Bake for 30 minutes. Carefully remove each strip to a cutting board and cut, somewhat diagonally, into ½" slices. Turn each slice onto its side and return to baking sheet. Continue baking another 15 minutes. Remove from pan and cool on a rack.

To coat with chocolate: melt chocolate over hot, not boiling, water; take care not to splash any water into chocolate. Dip one end, about ¼ to ⅓ of the cookie, into chocolate. Spread evenly and remove excess with small spatula. Place on waxed paper or parchment-lined cookie sheet and refrigerate to harden. Remove from paper and store in a tight container in a cool place.

Nutritional information per cookie without chocolate   119 calories, 6.2 grams fat, 1.8 grams saturated fat, 0.9 grams polyunsaturated fat, 3.1 grams monounsaturated fat, 3 grams protein, 15 grams carbohydrate, 1.4 grams fiber, 19 mg cholesterol, 56 mg sodium, 86 mg potassium

Nutritional information per cookie with chocolate   146 calories, 8 grams fat, 3 grams saturated fat, 1 gram polyunsaturated fat, 3.7 grams monounsaturated fat, 3 grams protein, 18 grams carbohydrate, 1.6 grams fiber, 19 mg cholesterol, 57 mg sodium, 110 mg potassium

*see **To Toast Nuts**, page 19

Sicilian Cheesecake
(Cassata alla Siciliana)
Italy

Servings: 12

By substituting a cocoa-powdered sugar dusting for a rich chocolate butter-cream frosting, this dessert qualifies as lean and luscious.

Sponge cake:
3 eggs, separated
½ cup sugar plus 2 tbs. sugar
1 tsp. grated orange peel **or** lemon peel
3 tbs. orange juice
1 cup all-purpose flour
1 tsp. baking powder

Filling:
22 ozs. part skim ricotta cheese
⅓ cup sugar
¾ cup candied fruit
⅓ cup almonds*, toasted, chopped **or** pistachios
½ cup semi-sweet chocolate, chopped **or** chips
½ cup orange liqueur, such as Strega, Triple Sec or Grand Marnier

Topping:
½ tbs. powdered sugar
½ tbs. cocoa, unsweetened

Preheat oven to 375°. Whisk egg whites until soft peaks form. Add 2 tbs. sugar and continue whisking until stiff but not dry. In a separate bowl, whisk egg yolks and ½ cup sugar until lemon-colored. Add peel and juice and blend well. Sift flour and baking powder together. Add to yolk mixture and blend in. Fold in whites. Turn into a greased 10″ springform pan. Bake for 15 to 20 minutes or until evenly browned and firm. Cool for 15 minutes on a rack; remove from pan to finish cooling. Using a long, serrated knife, separate into 3 or 4 even layers.

In a bowl, mix filling ingredients together. Spread ½ or ⅓ of filling on top of bottom layer; spread remaining filling on top of middle layer (or ⅓ on top of each of the two remaining layers). Place top layer on cake with browned side up. Dust with mixture of powdered sugar and cocoa. Refrigerate for several hours before serving.

Nutritional information per serving   217 calories, 10.4 grams fat, 4.9 grams saturated fat, 0.9 grams polyunsaturated fat, 4 grams monounsaturated fat, 10 grams protein, 49 grams carbohydrate, 1 gram fiber, 85 mg cholesterol, 153 mg sodium, 178 mg potassium

*see **To Toast Nuts**, page 19

Tomato Sauce (Marinara)
Italy

*This basic sauce is nice in **Eggplant Parmesan**, page 96, in **Lasagna**, page 91, or with pasta.*

1 tbs. olive oil
1 cup onion, chopped
2 cloves garlic, minced
1 (28 ozs.) can or 4 cups whole, peeled tomatoes
1 (6 ozs.) can tomato paste
1 tsp. basil
1 tsp. oregano

In a large saucepan, sauté onion and garlic in oil. Add tomatoes, crushing or chopping whole tomatoes into smaller pieces. Add tomato paste and seasonings. Simmer for 5 to 10 minutes to blend flavors, stirring frequently to prevent sticking.

Nutritional information per 1-cup serving   122 calories, 4.4 grams fat, 0.6 grams saturated fat, 0.7 grams polyunsaturated fat, 2.6 grams monounsaturated fat, 4 grams protein, 20 grams carbohydrate, 3.5 grams fiber, 0 mg cholesterol, 351 mg sodium, 918 mg potassium

Mexico

Now that the tortilla is ubiquitous throughout America, many Mexican dishes have dual citizenship.

Christmas Salad
Mexico

There are many variations of this recipe. Create your own by adding pineapple, substituting water chestnuts for jicama, or making other changes to suit your taste.

2 oranges, pared, sectioned
1 grapefruit, pared, sectioned
½ lb. jicama, peeled, cut into 1" long sticks
1 large black-skinned (Haas) avocado
½ cup pomegranate seeds* (one medium pomegranate)
4 lettuce leaf cups

Toss orange, grapefruit and jicama together in a bowl. To serve: using a slotted spoon, divide mixture among four lettuce cups. Peel, pit and slice avocado into bowl, turning to coat with citrus juices. Arrange slices on top of each salad. Sprinkle pomegranate seeds on top of each salad. Pour any remaining juices over salads.

Nutritional information per serving   154 calories, 7.7 grams fat, 1.1 grams saturated fat, 0.9 grams polyunsaturated fat, 4.9 grams monounsaturated fat, 3 grams protein, 22 grams carbohydrate, 3.8 grams fiber, 0 mg cholesterol, 27 mg sodium, 914 mg potassium

* To remove seeds from pomegranate: carefully cut fruit into quarters. Fill a bowl with water. Holding fruit sections underwater to prevent stains from juice, separate seeds from pith. Seeds will sink, allowing pith and peel to be discarded.

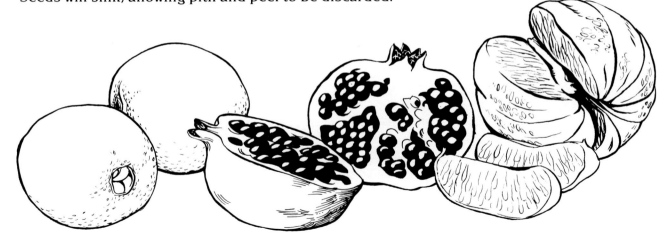

Taco Salad
Mexico

Servings: 12

This recipe makes a large salad. Invite your friends over for a fiesta. Olé!

1 head romaine lettuce, cut crosswise into ½" shred
6 cups **Beans with Green Chilies**, page 116
½ cup nonfat plain yogurt **or Yogurt Cheese**, page 46
2 cups **Salsa Fresca**, page 125
2 fresh tomatoes, cut into wedges
1 (4 ozs. drained weight) can ripe olives, sliced
1 large black-skinned avocado (Haas), sliced or cubed
4 ozs. cheddar cheese, grated
fresh cilantro sprigs (optional)
Tortilla Triangles* or tortilla chips to encircle edge of platter (optional)

Place shredded lettuce on a large oval platter or pasta serving plate. Arrange Beans with Green Chilies on top of lettuce. Spread yogurt in the center. Top with Salsa Fresca. Garnish with tomatoes, olives and avocado. Sprinkle cheese on top. Garnish with cilantro and Tortilla Triangles or chips, if desired.

114 Mexico

Nutritional information per serving   261 calories, 9.8 grams fat, 2.9 grams saturated fat, 1.5 grams polyunsaturated fat, 4.7 grams monounsaturated fat, 14 grams protein, 33 grams carbohydrate, 11.7 grams fiber, 10 mg cholesterol, 462 mg sodium, 1004 mg potassium

* To Make **Tortilla Triangles**: Use 1 pkg. whole wheat flour tortillas. Cut tortillas into wedges. Arrange pieces in a single layer on a baking sheet. Bake in 350° oven for 5 minutes. Turn over when browned on one side and bake an additional few minutes until browned and crisp.

Beans with Green Chilies

Mexico

These beans have enough character to stand up on their own, but they also pair up nicely with tortillas as burritos, tacos and tostadas.

1 lb. dried red beans **or**
  pintos **or** pinks
2 tsp. salt
10 cups water
1 tsp. salt
6 cups water
1 tbs. canola oil
1 cup onion, chopped
2 green onions, chopped

1 clove garlic, minced
1 (32 ozs.) can whole, peeled
  tomatoes with juice
1 (4 ozs.) can mild green chilies, diced
1-2 tbs. chili powder
¼ tsp. cumin
¼ tsp. oregano
½ tsp. salt

Sort beans. Add 2 tsp. salt and cover with 10 cups boiling water. Cover and soak for 1 to 4 hours. Drain. In a large pot, cover beans with 6 cups water and 1 tsp. salt; bring to a boil, cover and simmer for 1 to 1½ hours until done but still retaining shape. Drain. In a large saucepan, heat oil and cook onions and garlic until soft. Add tomatoes, chilies and seasonings. Simmer for 10 to 15 minutes to blend flavors. Add to beans and mix well. Serve alone or in **Taco Salad**, page 114.

Nutritional information per 1-cup serving 312 calories, 3.8 grams fat, 0.3 grams saturated fat, 1.5 grams polyunsaturated fat, 1.6 grams monounsaturated fat, 19 grams protein, 52 grams carbohydrate, 18.7 grams fiber, 0 mg cholesterol, 440 mg sodium, 1369 mg potassium

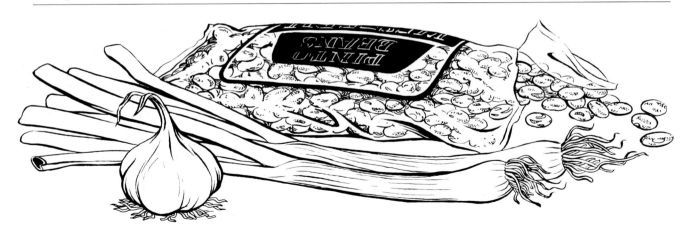

Avocado Dip/Spread (Light Guacamole)
Mexico

1½ cups

This lower fat version of the popular dip takes advantage of thickened yogurt as an extender.

1 green onion, chopped (2 tbs.)
1 large (8 ozs.) black-skinned
avocado (Haas variety)
3 tbs. fresh lime juice (one lime)
½ cup plain nonfat **Yogurt Cheese**,
page 46

¼ tsp. salt
3 drops Tabasco sauce, or to taste
3 cherry tomatoes (optional)
¼ cup red bell pepper (optional)
1 tbs. fresh cilantro (optional)

Chop onion in a food processor. Add avocado, lime, yogurt and seasonings and pulse just until avocado is mashed coarsely. Add remaining ingredients, if used; pulse several times to mix together. Serve with oven-toasted **Tortilla Triangles**, page 115, raw vegetable pieces or as a sandwich filling.

Nutritional information per 3 tbs. 64 calories, 4.9 grams fat, 0.7 grams saturated fat, 0.6 grams polyunsaturated fat, 3.2 grams monounsaturated fat, 2 grams protein, 4 grams carbohydrate, 0.9 grams fiber, 1 mg cholesterol, 84 mg sodium, 237 mg potassium

Greek Salad (page 142) ▶

Refried Beans (Frijoles Refritos)
Mexico

These "nonfried" beans vary from the typical version in that they are not fried repeatedly in lard. Use them in burritos, tostadas, enchiladas or as a side dish with a sprinkle of grated Monterey Jack cheese melted on top.

1 tbs. olive oil
1 cup onions, chopped
4 cloves garlic, minced
3 (15 ozs. each) cans pinto beans, drained **or**
   1 lb. dried pintos, cooked and drained
1 (28 ozs.) can whole, peeled tomatoes, drained

1½ tsp. cumin
1 tsp. chili powder
¼ tsp. cayenne pepper
½ tsp. salt

In a large, high-sided skillet, sauté onion in oil until soft. Add garlic, beans, tomatoes, cumin, chili, pepper and salt. Using a potato masher or large fork, break up the beans and tomatoes until only slightly lumpy.

Nutritional information per ½ cup serving 165 calories, 2.1 grams fat, 0.3 grams saturated fat, 0.5 grams polyunsaturated fat, 1.1 grams monounsaturated fat, 8 grams protein, 29 grams carbohydrate, 10.6 grams fiber, 0 mg cholesterol, 204 mg sodium, 606 mg potassium

Super Tostada (page 128) with Refried Beans (page 121)
◄ **and Fresh Hot Sauce (page 125)**

Poultry Enchiladas

Servings: 10

Mexico

*These enchiladas are easily converted to "vegetarian" by substituting a seasoned rice, such as **Brazilian Rice**, page 161, for the chicken.*

Sauce:
1 tbs. canola oil
1½ cups onion, chopped
3 cloves garlic, minced
3 jalapeno chili peppers*, finely chopped **or** 3 tsp. canned or bottled
1 tsp. salt
1 (28 ozs.) can whole, peeled tomatoes, juice included
1 (16 ozs.) can tomato sauce
3 tsp. chili powder

In a large skillet, lightly sauté onion in oil until soft. Add remaining ingredients, breaking up tomatoes with a spoon. Simmer for 15 to 20 minutes to blend flavors.

Filling:

2 cups boneless cooked chicken, shredded or cut into large cubes (see **Chicken and Stock**, page 28) **or** turkey

½ cup green onion, chopped

1 (6 ozs. drained weight) can ripe olives, drained, coarsely chopped (use half in filling; reserve half for topping)

1 (15 ozs.) can kidney beans, drained, chopped **or**
   1½ cups **Refried Beans**, page 121

2 tsp. chili powder

½ tsp. salt

¼ cup fresh cilantro, chopped

Mix filling ingredients together in a large bowl. (If Refried Beans are used, keep these separate and spread them onto tortilla before the filling.) Add ⅓ of the sauce to filling and blend together.

10 large whole wheat **or** flour tortillas

6 ozs. cheddar cheese, grated

To assemble: put ½ cup sauce in bottom of a 9" x 13" glass casserole. Place 1/10 of filling on tortilla and roll up. (Or spread 1/10 Refried Beans on tortilla, add filling mixture and roll up.) Place seam side down on sauce in dish. Repeat with remaining tortillas and filling, placing each rolled enchilada snugly next to the others. Sprinkle half of cheese on tortillas; top with sauce, remaining olives and remaining cheese. Cover tightly and bake at 350° for 30 minutes; uncover and bake 15 minutes longer or until bubbly.

Nutritional information per enchilada   398 calories, 17 grams fat, 5.4 grams saturated fat, 3.1 grams polyunsaturated fat, 7.3 grams monounsaturated fat, 21 grams protein, 47 grams carbohydrate, 6.2 grams fiber, 40 mg cholesterol, 1347 mg sodium, 647 mg potassium

---

* see **To Handle Fresh Chilies**, page 17

Fresh Hot Sauce (Salsa Fresca)
Mexico

2 cups

Enjoy this as a dip or topping. Uncooked, it retains a tantalizing freshness and crispness.

1 cup onion, finely chopped
1 lb. tomatoes, peeled, chopped (2 tomatoes)
1-2 fresh jalapeno chilies,* minced **or** 1-2 tsp. canned or bottled
¼ cup fresh cilantro, chopped
¼ cup fresh lemon juice (1 lemon)
½ tsp. salt
freshly ground pepper

Mix all ingredients together. Store covered in refrigerator up to 7 days.

Nutritional information per ¼ cup 21 calories, 0.2 grams fat, 0 grams saturated fat, 0.1 grams polyunsaturated fat, 0 grams monounsaturated fat, 1 gram protein, 5 grams carbohydrate, 1.4 grams fiber, 0 mg cholesterol, 149 mg sodium, 169 mg potassium

* see **To Handle Fresh Chilies**, page 17

Red Snapper Veracruz
Mexico

You can use fresh or canned chilies in this recipe. I find the canned ones more predictable in terms of "temperature." Traditionally this dish is served with small, boiled potatoes dusted with chopped parsley.

1 tsp. olive oil
½ cup onions, chopped
2 cups fresh tomatoes, peeled, coarsely chopped (3 tomatoes) **or**
   1 (16 ozs.) can Italian plum tomatoes, drained
2 cloves garlic, minced
3 tsp. canned jalapeno chilies, minced **or**
   3 fresh chilies,* minced
¼ cup pimiento-stuffed olives, coarsely chopped
1 tbs. fresh lime juice
½ tsp. salt
freshly ground pepper
2 tbs. all-purpose flour
1 lb. red snapper (4 small fillets)
1 tbs. olive oil

In a medium saucepan, cook onions in oil until soft. Add tomatoes and seasonings. Cook over moderate heat, uncovered, about 10 to 15 minutes. Place flour in a brown paper bag; add fish and shake, coating fillets completely. Shake off any excess flour. In a large skillet, heat 1 tbs. oil and sauté fish, cooking only a couple of minutes on each side until just done. Serve hot with sauce covering half of each fish portion.

Nutritional information per serving   221 calories, 8.7 grams fat, 1.4 grams saturated fat, 1.4 grams polyunsaturated fat, 5 grams monounsaturated fat, 29 grams protein, 10 grams carbohydrate, 2.6 grams fiber, 68 mg cholesterol, 674 mg sodium, 795 mg potassium

* see **To Handle Fresh Chilies**, page 17

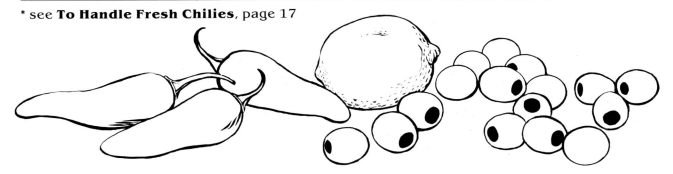

Super Tostada (Tostada de Lujo)

Mexico

Servings: 1

This "open-face sandwich" is magnifico! Definitely a meal by itself. Far lower in fat than any tostada you can order in a restaurant, it can be lower still if you omit the cheese.

1 whole wheat, flour, or corn tortilla
½ cup **Refried Beans**, page 121, warmed
2 ozs. boneless cooked chicken (see **Chicken and Stock**, page 28),
    shredded or diced **or** cooked turkey, beef or pork **or**
    (vegetarian version) ½ cup warmed **Brazilian Rice**, page 161
1 cup romaine lettuce, cut crosswise into ½" wide shred
2 tbs. nonfat plain yogurt
3 slices avocado (¼ avocado) **or** 2 tbs. **Light Guacamole**, page 118
½ oz. cheddar cheese, grated
¼ cup **Salsa Fresca**, page 125

To crisp tortilla, preheat oven to 450°. Place whole wheat or flour tortilla on oven rack and heat 3 to 5 minutes, turning once. If corn tortilla is used, run quickly under water from the faucet, shaking off excess. Place on rack in 350° oven for about 10 minutes, turning once. To serve, place tortilla on plate, spread beans to within 1" of the edge, and layer remaining ingredients on top in the order listed.

Nutritional information per tostada 603 Calories, 21.4 grams fat, 5.8 grams saturated fat, 3.8 grams polyunsaturated fat, 9.9 grams monounsaturated fat, 37 grams protein, 71 grams carbohydrate, 15.4 grams fiber, 59 mg cholesterol, 725 mg sodium, 1456 mg potassium

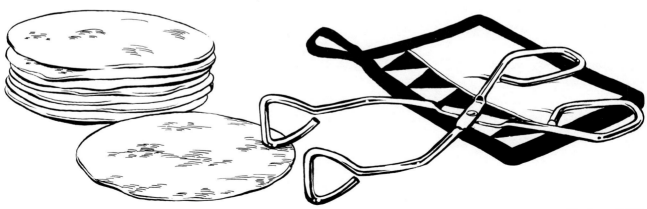

Caramel Topped Custard (Flan)
Mexico

The caramelized sugar turns a simple custard into an elegant presentation.

½ cup sugar
¼ cup water
3 eggs, **or** 2 eggs and 2 egg whites
¼ cup sugar **or** 3 tbs. honey

¼ tsp. salt
½ tsp. vanilla
2 cups nonfat milk

Preheat oven to 325°. Set a baking pan with 1" of water in oven to preheat. In a heavy, small saucepan, heat sugar and water over medium-high heat, stirring with a flat wooden utensil, until it carmelizes into a golden brown syrup. Watch very carefully toward the end to prevent scorching. Also, be very careful; molten sugar is very hot. Immediately pour the caramel into a flat-bottomed heatproof 1½-quart casserole (or six 5-ounce individual custard cups), tipping to coat bottom and sides before it hardens. (Caramel will ``melt'' once the custard is cooked and chilled.)

In a large bowl, whisk eggs, sugar, salt and vanilla together. Mix in milk. Pour custard into casserole on top of caramel. Place in water bath in oven and bake about 45 minutes, or until a table knife inserted into custard comes out clean. Remove casserole from water bath and cool on rack. Remove water bath from oven carefully; discard water. Chill custard in refrigerator at least 3 hours. To serve, loosen edge and turn upside down onto serving plate. Pour any caramel remaining in dish over the custard.

Nutritional information per serving   164 calories, 2.9 grams fat, 0.9 grams saturated fat, 0.4 grams polyunsaturated fat, 1.2 grams monounsaturated fat, 6 grams protein, 29 grams carbohydrate, 0 grams fiber, 138 mg cholesterol, 166 mg sodium, 169 mg potassium

Middle East

Claimed by some to be the healthiest cuisine in the world (all those vegetables, beans and olive oil), these foods come from Armenia, Greece, India, Israel and other Middle Eastern countries.

Garbanzo Bean Spread (Hummus)

Middle East

A favorite in the Arab states for centuries, this combination of flavors continues to please as a dip or spread.

⅓ cup sesame seeds
3 cloves garlic
1 (15 oz.) can **or** 1½ cups cooked
   garbanzo beans, partially drained;
   reserve ¼ cup liquid

3 tbs. lemon juice (1 small lemon)
½ tsp. cumin
½ tsp. salt
½ cup (loosely packed) parsley tops
dash of cayenne pepper (optional)

Blend sesame seeds in a food processor until smooth. Add garlic, beans, liquid, lemon and salt. Puree smooth. Add parsley and mix just enough to chop coarsely. Serve on wedges of pita bread garnished with parsley, if desired.

Nutritional information per ¼ cup   121 calories, 5.5 grams fat, 0.7 grams saturated fat, 2.5 grams polyunsaturated fat, 1.9 grams monounsaturated fat, 6 grams protein, 13 grams carbohydrate, 2.9 grams fiber, 0 mg cholesterol, 185 mg sodium, 188 mg potassium

Stuffed Grape Leaves (Dolmas)
Greece

24 dolmas

Whether you call these leaf-wrapped finger-foods dolmas, dolmehs, or dolmathes, they are a favorite appetizer or snack.

1 tbs. olive oil
1 cup onion, finely chopped
⅓ cup long grain converted rice
¾ cup water
¼ tsp. allspice
½ tsp. salt
freshly ground pepper

2 tbs. pine nuts*, lightly toasted
2 tbs. dried currants
30 preserved grape leaves
   (½ contents of 8 oz. jar)
¼ cup water
plain nonfat yogurt (optional)
lemon wedges (optional)

In a heavy skillet with a tight-fitting lid, heat oil over moderately high heat; sauté onion until soft but not browned. Add rice and stir about one minute. Add water, allspice, salt and pepper; bring to a boil, cover, reduce heat to simmer and cook 25 minutes, until rice is tender and all water is absorbed. Stir in pine nuts and currants. To prepare dolmas: remove grape leaves to be used from jar. Add water to brine in jar, covering remaining leaves. Reserve for another time. Separate removed leaves. Rinse and place on paper towels to drain. Prepare a 1-quart glass or nonreactive dish by lining bottom with several of the smaller leaves. To roll dolma: spread leaf flat with dull or veined side up; cut off any stem. Place 1 tbs. filling on stem end of leaf, roll once, fold each side into middle and roll into a cylinder. Arrange seam side down, side by side in dish. Arrange extra, smaller leaves on top of each layer. When all dolmas are rolled, add water to dish, cover tightly and cook in a 350° oven for 50 minutes. Let cool, covered. Serve at room temperature, accompanied with lemon wedges and yogurt for dipping, if desired.

Nutritional information per dolma 25 calories, 1.1 grams fat, 0.2 grams saturated fat, 0.3 grams polyunsaturated fat, 0.6 grams monounsaturated fat, 1 gram protein, 4 grams carbohydrate, 0.4 grams fiber, 0 mg cholesterol, 46 mg sodium, 60 mg potassium

*see **To Toast Nuts**, page 19

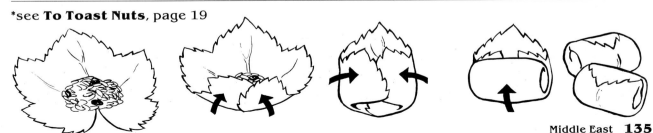

Eggplant Spread (Baba Ghannooj)
Middle East

2½ cups

This nippy dip goes well with raw vegetable sticks or is an interesting sandwich filling, especially in pocket bread.

1½ lb. eggplant (1 medium)
⅓ cup sesame seeds
2 cloves garlic

¼ cup fresh lemon juice (1 lemon)
1 tsp. salt
¼ tsp. cumin

Bake the whole eggplant in a 350° oven for 1 hour and 15 minutes, until very tender. Remove from oven and let cool for 15 minutes. (Microwave alternative — but this won't have the ''roasted'' flavor of oven-baked — pierce eggplant; cook, covered, 20 minutes at 70% or until tender.) Cut off stem end and remove peel. Puree sesame seeds until smooth in a food processor. Add garlic, lemon and seasonings. Add eggplant; blend until smooth.

Nutritional information per ¼ cup 50 calories, 2.8 grams fat, 0.4 grams saturated fat, 1.2 grams polyunsaturated fat, 1 gram monounsaturated fat, 2 grams protein, 6 grams carbohydrate, 2.7 grams fiber, 0 mg cholesterol, 218 mg sodium, 181 mg potassium

Bulgur Pilaf
Middle East

Servings: 8

This simple side dish offers a nice alternative to rice. Accompany with yogurt, if desired.

1 tbs. olive oil
½ cup onion, chopped
2 ozs. (about ½ cup) vermicelli noodles broken into 1" lengths
3½ cups hot water
1½ cups bulgur (processed cracked wheat)
1 tsp. salt
freshly ground pepper

In a large skillet with a lid, sauté onion in oil until soft. Add vermicelli pieces and sauté with onion, browning lightly. Add bulgur, water and seasonings. Bring to a boil, cover and reduce heat to simmer. Cook, without opening, 10 minutes. Turn off heat, leaving cover on, and allow to stand 20 minutes longer. Fluff with a fork and serve hot.

Nutritional information per serving   157 calories, 2.3 grams fat, 0.5 grams saturated fat, 0.4 grams polyunsaturated fat, 1.3 grams monounsaturated fat, 5 grams protein, 30 grams carbohydrate, 3.3 grams fiber, 0 mg cholesterol, 268 mg sodium, 102 mg potassium

Egg and Lemon Soup
(Soupa Avgolemono)
Greece

Servings: 4

Light, lemony and luscious!

4 cups chicken stock (see **Chicken and Stock**, page 28) **or**
    4 cups water plus 4 tsp. instant chicken-flavored bouillon
¼ cup brown rice **or** converted white rice
2 eggs
2 tbs. fresh lemon juice
2 tbs. fresh mint, minced **or** 2 tsp. dried mint
½ tsp. salt
lemon slices and mint sprigs

In a medium saucepan, bring chicken stock to a boil. Add rice, cover, reduce heat to simmer and cook for 40 minutes (20 minutes, if white rice). In a small bowl, beat eggs with lemon, mint and salt. When rice is tender, dip out ½ cup of liquid and add to egg mixture, whisking well. Add egg mixture to hot soup, stirring constantly. Do not boil (egg will curdle) but heat until mixture thickens slightly. Serve immediately, garnished with thin lemon slices and a sprig of fresh mint, if desired.

Nutritional information per serving   122 calories, 4.4 grams fat, 1.3 grams saturated fat, 0.7 grams polyunsaturated fat, 1.8 grams monounsaturated fat, 9 grams protein, 11 grams carbohydrate, 0.5 grams fiber, 138 mg cholesterol, 1078 mg sodium, 277 mg potassium

Greek Salad

Greece

This salad needs a patio with summery breezes, a crusty loaf of just-baked bread, a chilled bottle of wine and "thou."

6 cups romaine lettuce (1 medium head), torn into bite-sized pieces
1 clove garlic, cut
2 medium tomatoes, cut into wedges **or** 2 cups cherry tomatoes
1 medium cucumber, peeled, sliced
1 green pepper, seeded, sliced
2 green onions, chopped
2 ozs. feta cheese, cubed or crumbled
12 Greek olives **or** black olives
1 oz. flat anchovy fillets (4 fillets), drained

Dressing:
2 tbs. extra virgin olive oil
3 tbs. fresh lemon juice
¼ tsp. oregano

¼ tsp. mint (optional)
1 tsp. capers, drained (optional)
freshly ground pepper

Rub salad bowl or platter with cut clove of garlic. Whisk dressing ingredients together in a small bowl. Compose salad artistically on a bed of lettuce and drizzle dressing on top **or** toss salad ingredients together, adding dressing at the end.

Nutritional information per serving   175 calories, 14 grams fat, 3.8 grams saturated fat, 1.4 grams polyunsaturated fat, 7.8 grams monounsaturated fat, 6 grams protein, 10 grams carbohydrate, 4.4 grams fiber, 18 mg cholesterol, 281 mg sodium, 561 mg potassium

Spiced Basmati Rice
Middle East

Servings: 6

*Curry dishes pair nicely with fruited rice. This also goes well with **Shish Kebab**, page 148 .*

1 tbs. canola oil
½ cup onion, thinly sliced
1 cup long-grain uncooked basmati rice, brown **or** white
2 cups chicken stock **or** 2 cups water and 2 tsp. instant
　chicken-flavored bouillon (see **Chicken and Stock**, page 28)
1 tsp. salt (omit if bouillon is used)
2 tbs. unsalted cashews*, toasted, coarsely chopped
2 tbs. unsalted almonds, toasted, coarsely chopped
2 tbs. pine nuts
¼ cup raisins
¼ tsp. nutmeg
¼ tsp. cinnamon
⅛ tsp. cardamom
freshly ground pepper

In a large skillet, heat oil and sauté onion until soft. Add rice and cook 2 to 3 minutes, stirring constantly. In a medium saucepan, heat stock to boiling, add salt and rice-onion mixture. Bring to a boil, cover, reduce heat, and simmer 45 minutes (or 20 for white rice). Turn cooked rice into a serving casserole; toss with nuts, raisins and spices. Season to taste. Serve hot.

Nutritional information per serving   220 calories, 8.1 grams fat, 1.2 grams saturated fat, 2.3 grams polyunsaturated fat, 4.3 grams monounsaturated fat, 6 grams protein, 32 grams carbohydrate, 2.4 grams fiber, 0 mg cholesterol, 619 mg sodium, 262 mg potassium

*see **To Toast Nuts**, page 19

Roasted Chicken with Yogurt (Tandoori Murghi)
India

Servings:4

Turmeric is a tropical plant in the ginger family. It is the basis of Indian curry blends. Powder made from the root portion ranges in color from light golden yellow to dark orange; it gives a rich color to this dish.

3 lbs. chicken breasts
¼ cup fresh lemon juice **or** lime juice
1 cup nonfat plain yogurt
1" fresh ginger root, peeled, minced
2 cloves garlic, minced
1 tsp. coriander seed, ground **or** ½ tsp coriander
½ tsp. cumin seed, ground **or** ¼ tsp. cumin
½ tsp. salt
¼ tsp. cayenne pepper **or** 1 small fresh green chili,* chopped
½ tsp. turmeric (optional) **or** ½ tsp. saffron threads (optional)
lime slices (optional)

Remove skin from chicken breasts. In a nonreactive glass or plastic container, mix together remaining ingredients for marinade. If using saffron, soak threads in 2 tbs. boiling water 5 to 10 minutes; strain, adding liquid to marinade, and discard threads. Submerge chicken pieces in marinade; cover; refrigerate, turning occasionally, 8 to 24 hours. Bake, covered with marinade, in a roasting pan in 350° oven for 45 minutes or until juices run clear when chicken is pierced with a sharp fork. Garnish with lime slices, if desired.

Nutritional information per serving 166 calories, 1.7 grams fat, 0.5 grams saturated fat, 0.4 grams polyunsaturated fat, 0.4 grams monounsaturated fat, 30 grams protein, 7 grams carbohydrate, 0.3 grams fiber, 66 mg cholesterol, 384 mg sodium, 480 mg potassium

* see **To Handle Fresh Chilies**, page 17

Skewered Grilled Lamb (Shish Kebab)

Servings: 8

Middle East

Serve this in pita bread with chopped tomato and raw onion or alongside **Bulgur Pilaf**, *page 139 , or* **Spiced Basmati Rice**, *page 144.*

1 lb. lean boneless leg of lamb cut into 1" cubes **or** lean boneless beef

Marinade:

1 tbs. olive oil
3 tbs. fresh lemon juice
3 tbs. red wine
1 clove garlic, minced

½ tsp. oregano
½ tsp. rosemary
½ tsp. salt
½ tsp. pepper

Vegetables:

1 green bell pepper, cut into 1" squares
1 onion, cut into six wedges, pieces separated
1 lb. (1 basket) cherry tomatoes

In a nonreactive bowl, mix together marinade and toss with lamb cubes. Cover and refrigerate, marinating overnight. Turn several times to season evenly. Thread lamb and vegetables onto 8 large skewers. Broil 3" from heat or grill over charcoal until meat is pink in center, about 15 minutes. Turn and baste with marinade every 5 minutes.

Nutritional information per serving   146 calories, 6.6 grams fat, 2.1 grams saturated fat, 0.6 grams polyunsaturated fat, 3 grams monounsaturated fat, 16 grams protein, 5 grams carbohydrate, 1.4 grams fiber, 51 mg cholesterol, 177 mg sodium, 369 mg potassium

Jewish Egg Bread (Challah)
Israel

In ancient times, a small piece of the challah dough was given as an offering or tithe. Although a valuable food whether made from whole wheat or white flour, I prefer the flavor and texture of the wholegrain version offered here. Be sure to braid the loaf.

1 tbs. dry active yeast
1 tsp. sugar
½ cup warm water (105°-115°)
3 eggs
3 tbs. oil
2 tsp. salt

1 tbs. sugar
5 cups whole wheat flour, very finely ground
¾ cup water
pinch of saffron to enrich color (optional)
½ egg, beaten with 1 tbs. water
½ tbs. poppy seed

Proof yeast in sweetened water. In a large mixer bowl, mix eggs, oil, salt, sugar, flour, water and saffron, if used. Add foamy yeast. Knead 5 to 7 minutes. Place in a greased bowl; cover with plastic. Let rise 60 minutes. Punch down; let rest 5 minutes. Divide dough into four pieces, each 22" long and wider in the middle than at the ends. Working on a large baking sheet, braid pieces of dough into one loaf (see diagram). Let rise 45 minutes, covered with plastic wrap. Glaze with egg-water mixture and sprinkle with poppy seeds. Bake at 375° for 15 minutes; reduce heat to 350° and bake an additional 15 minutes.

__Nutritional information per slice__ 110 calories, 3 grams fat, 0.4 grams saturated fat, 0.9 grams polyunsaturated fat, 1.4 grams monounsaturated fat, 4 grams protein, 18 grams carbohydrate, 2.7 grams fiber, 34 mg cholesterol, 187 mg sodium, 109 mg potassium

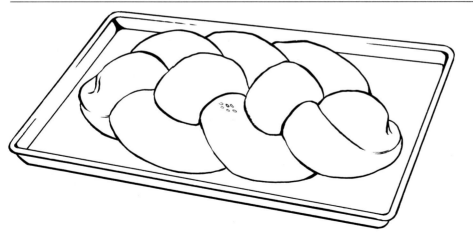

From one side weave over, then under. From the other side weave under, then over.

Honey Cake
Israel

Servings: 16

This cake is somewhat like a pound cake, except it does not contain a pound of butter!! It is a special favorite during Jewish holidays.

¼ cup canola oil
1 cup honey
3 egg yolks
2 tsp. grated orange peel **or** lemon peel
2 cups all-purpose flour
½ tsp. cinnamon
½ tsp. allspice
⅛ tsp. cloves
1½ tsp. baking powder
1 tsp. baking soda
½ tsp. salt
⅔ cup double-strength coffee, room temperature **or** 1 tbs.
   instant coffee dissolved in ¼ cup boiling water; add cool water to make ⅔ cup
3 egg whites

¼ cup dried currants **or** raisins
15-20 whole almonds (optional)

Preheat oven to 325°. Grease and flour a 9" x 5" x 3" loaf pan. In a large mixer bowl, beat oil and honey together. Add yolks and peel and beat well. Sift dry ingredients together. In a separate bowl, whisk egg whites until soft peaks form. Add dry ingredients alternately with coffee to a large mixer bowl, beating only enough to blend well. Add currants. Fold beaten egg whites into cake mixture. Turn batter into prepared pan. Decorate top of cake with almonds, if desired. Bake 60 minutes or until broomstraw or toothpick inserted into center of cake comes out clean. Cool 5 to 10 minutes in pan, and remove to rack to finish cooling.

Nutritional information per serving   174 calories, 4.6 grams fat, 0.5 grams saturated fat, 1.2 grams polyunsaturated fat, 2.6 grams monounsaturated fat, 3 grams protein, 32 grams carbohydrate, 0.6 grams fiber, 51 mg cholesterol, 164 mg sodium, 68 mg potassium

Spain, Portugal, South America and the Caribbean

The Spanish and Portuguese travelled widely, introducing favored foods to South America and the Carribbean region.

Shellfish in Papaya Boats (page 162) ▶

Cold Tomato Soup (Gaspacho)

Servings: 4

Spain

This is a great starter for a patio barbecue meal. Add a pitcher of sangria and you have a party.

1½ lbs. fresh tomatoes, peeled
2 cloves garlic
2 tbs. red wine vinegar
1 tbs. olive oil
1 cup (loosely packed) crumbled soft white
    bread, crusts removed (sourdough is nice)
1 cucumber, peeled, chopped

1 onion, chopped
1 green pepper, chopped
½ tsp. salt
freshly ground pepper
4 slices bread, cubed,
    toasted into croutons

Puree tomatoes, garlic, vinegar, oil and bread in a food processor. Add ⅓ cup **each** cucumber, onion and green pepper to tomato mixture and continue processing until smooth. Reserve remaining cucumber, onion and pepper to serve separately, along with croutons, for garnish. Season soup. Chill at least 3 hours. Serve in chilled soup plates or bowls.

Nutritional information per serving (including 1 tbs. each of three vegetables and 1 slice of bread as croutons) 222 calories, 4.9 grams fat, 0.8 grams saturated fat, 0.8 grams polyunsaturated fat, 2.7 grams monounsaturated fat, 7 grams protein, 40 grams carbohydrate, 6.6 grams fiber, 0 mg cholesterol, 519 mg sodium, 816 mg potassium

---

Black Bean Salad
Caribbean

Servings: 6

Give this salad the spotlight; surround it with hot crusty bread and fresh fruit and you have a dramatic, delicious meal.

1 lb. black beans, dry
10 cups water
1 tsp. salt
6 cups water
1 tsp. salt
1 bay leaf
½ tsp. thyme
½ cup red onion, chopped
½ cup green bell pepper, finely diced
½ cup red bell pepper, finely diced
½ cup yellow bell pepper,
   finely diced

2 fresh jalapeno peppers*, minced **or**
   2-3 tsp. canned or bottled
3 tbs. fresh cilantro, chopped
¼ cup olive oil
2 tbs. white wine vinegar
3 tbs. orange juice
2 tsp. grated orange peel
2 cloves garlic, minced
½ tsp. cumin seeds, crushed **or**
   coriander seeds, crushed
½ tsp. salt
freshly ground pepper

Sort and wash beans. To soak: cover with 10 cups of water, add salt, heat to boiling, boil 1 to 2 minutes, cover and let stand one hour. Drain. To cook: cover with 6 cups of water, add salt, bay leaf and thyme, bring to a boil, reduce heat, partially cover and simmer 40 to 50 minutes until beans are tender but not mushy. Drain and discard bay leaf. In a large bowl, toss beans with bell peppers, jalapenos and cilantro. Mix remaining ingredients together for dressing and pour over beans and peppers. Toss lightly until well mixed. Chill or serve warm, garnished with bell pepper rings, cilantro sprigs and nonfat, plain **Yogurt Cheese,** page 46, on top or to pass, if desired.

Nutritional information per serving   283 calories, 9.8 grams fat, 1.3 grams saturated fat, 1.3 grams polyunsaturated fat, 6.7 grams monounsaturated fat, 13 grams protein, 38 grams carbohydrate, 13.6 grams fiber, 0 mg cholesterol, 372 mg sodium, 609 mg potassium

---

* see **To Handle Fresh Chilies**, page 17

Chard and Sausage Soup (Caldo Verde)

Servings: 6

Portugal

This wonderful soup, although originally from Portugal, has travelled extensively and established itself as a favorite throughout the new world.

4 ozs. linguica **or** chorizo or other
  garlic-smoked pork sausage
1 lb. potatoes, peeled, diced
  (2 medium-large potatoes)

6 cups water
1½ tsp. salt
½ lb. fresh chard
freshly ground pepper

Remove outer skin from sausage. Place in a small saucepan, cover with water and simmer 20 minutes. In a large saucepan, cook potatoes in boiling, salted water, uncovered, until very soft, about 20 minutes. Using a potato masher or large wooden spoon, mash potatoes against bottom or side of pan. Stack chard leaves together. Slice crosswise into very thin shreds, about ⅛". Add to potato broth; cook, uncovered, 10 minutes. Drain sausage; slice thinly or chop coarsely and add to soup. Season to taste. Serve hot.

Nutritional information per 1-cup serving 134 calories, 5.7 grams fat, 2 grams saturated fat, 0.7 grams polyunsaturated fat, 2.6 grams monounsaturated fat, 5 grams protein, 17 grams carbohydrate, 1.3 grams fiber, 14 mg cholesterol, 785 mg sodium, 436 mg potassium

Brazilian Rice
Brazil

This mildly seasoned rice complements bean and meat dishes.

2 cups chicken stock (see **Chicken and Stock**, page 28) **or** beef stock or 2 cups water plus 2 tsp. instant bouillon
1 cup long grain brown rice **or** converted white rice
1 tsp. salt
1 tsp. olive oil

½ cup onion, chopped
½ cup fresh tomatoes, peeled, chopped, **or** canned Italian plum tomatoes, drained
salt and pepper to taste
cilantro sprigs (optional)

In a medium saucepan, bring stock to a boil; add rice and salt. Cover tightly and simmer 45 minutes (or 25 minutes if white rice is used). In a sauté pan, cook onion lightly in oil. Add tomatoes and cook, reducing until very little liquid remains. Add vegetable mixture to rice, tossing to mix. Adjust seasoning to taste. Garnish with fresh cilantro sprigs, if desired.

Nutritional information per serving 188 calories, 2.1 grams fat, 0.4 grams saturated fat, 0.4 grams polyunsaturated fat, 1.1 grams monounsaturated fat, 4 grams protein, 38 grams carbohydrate, 2.4 grams fiber, 0 mg cholesterol, 539 mg sodium, 177 mg potassium

Shellfish in Papaya Boats
Caribbean

Servings: 4

Served on a warm night, with breezes wafting through open windows, this dish will transport you to the tropics.

1 tsp. canola oil
½ lb. medium shrimp, raw, in shells
1 tsp. canola oil
½ lb. fresh sea scallops **or**
  bay scallops
3 tbs. fresh lime juice (1 lime)
1 tsp. ginger root, minced

1 clove garlic, minced
¼ cup green onion, chopped
¼ cup fresh cilantro, chopped
2 fresh papayas, halved, seeded, peeled
lime wedges
cilantro sprigs (optional)

In a large skillet, sauté shrimp in 1 tsp. oil, just until they turn pink. Turn into a colander and rinse with cold water to stop cooking. Peel shrimp and remove tails. Add remaining teaspoon of oil to skillet and sauté scallops just until they lose their translucence. Remove from pan and reserve with shrimp. Deglaze pan with lime juice (dissolve small particles of sautéed shellfish on bottom of pan); add ginger, garlic and onion to skillet and cook briefly, blending flavors.

Remove from heat. Add shellfish and cilantro to seasonings in skillet and mix together. Cut a thin piece from the bottom of each papaya half to prevent tipping. Divide seasoned seafood among four papaya ``boats;'' serve with lime wedges as an entree or salad. Garnish with sprigs of cilantro, if desired.

__Nutritional information per serving__   210 calories, 4.2 grams fat, 0.6 grams saturated fat, 1.4 grams polyunsaturated fat, 1.8 grams monounsaturated fat, 28 grams protein, 19 grams carbohydrate, 3.1 grams fiber, 113 mg cholesterol, 258 mg sodium, 958 mg potassium

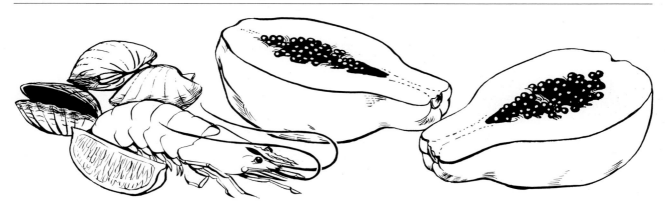

Salvadoran Seafood Stew
(Moqueca de Peixe)

Brazil

It is traditional to float red palm oil (dende oil) on top of this stew. Having already pushed the saturated fat limit with the coconut milk, I have excluded the palm oil flourish.

1 lb. fish fillets (red snapper, sea bass, etc.) **or**
  prawns, raw, shells removed **or** crab, shelled
¼ cup fresh lemon juice (one lemon)
1 (15 ozs.) can peeled tomatoes, juice included
1 cup onion, sliced
1 green pepper, sliced
2 cloves garlic, minced
2 green onions, cut crosswise into 4 parts, then sliced lengthwise
½ cup coconut milk*
½ tsp. salt
freshly ground pepper
½ cup fresh cilantro, chopped (one bunch)

Place fish in one layer in a large skillet. Cover with remaining ingredients, except cilantro. Simmer, covered, about 10 minutes. Add cilantro. Remove from heat and serve hot in soup plates accompanied with hot, crusty bread.

Nutritional information per serving   240 calories, 9.4 grams fat, 7 grams saturated fat, 1.1 grams polyunsaturated fat, 0.7 grams monounsaturated fat, 30 grams protein, 13 grams carbohydrate, 2.7 grams fiber, 68 mg cholesterol, 508 mg sodium, 1045 mg potassium

---

*To make coconut milk: purchase a fresh coconut which is full of liquid when shaken and has smooth, dark eyes. Puncture two of the three eyes by hammering a screwdriver into them. Drain away the liquid from the center. Freeze the whole coconut. Place the whole coconut in a preheated 350° oven until it cracks, no longer than 15 minutes. Split the shell further, if necessary, with a sharp blow of the hammer. If the shell does not fall away from coconut meat, pry it loose with the tip of a sharp knife. Leaving the outer brown skin on the coconut meat, grate it in a food processor (or by hand). Add one cup of very hot water and mix well. Place wet coconut in a cotton or linen towel and wring the liquid into a bowl. This is the coconut milk. Makes about 1 cup milk.

Portuguese Sweet Bread
(Pao Doce)
Portugal

2 loaves, 16 slices each

Often coiled into a snail shape or braided, this bread is sweet enough for a simple dessert.

1 tbs. active dry yeast
1 tsp. sugar
1 cup water (105°-115°)
3 eggs
1 cup sugar
⅓ cup canola oil

1 tsp. salt
⅓ cup instant nonfat milk powder
⅓ cup water
6 cups whole wheat flour, very finely ground **or** all-purpose flour
1 egg, lightly beaten (optional)

Mix yeast in sweetened warm water and let stand until foamy. In a large mixer bowl, mix eggs, sugar, oil, salt, milk powder and water. Blend thoroughly. Add proofed yeast and flour. Knead, using dough hook, 5 to 7 minutes. Dough will be very sticky. Turn dough into a greased bowl; cover with plastic; allow to rise one hour or until doubled in size. Punch down. Divide dough into two equal portions and shape into round loaves, about 6" across. (Loaves can also be coiled into snail or braid shapes.) Place in 8" or 9" pie plates, cover with plastic, and allow to rise again, about 45 minutes. Preheat oven to 350°. Brush loaves with beaten egg, if desired, and bake 35 to 40 minutes. Loaves will be richly browned. Remove from pie plates and cool on rack.

Nutritional information per slice   129 calories, 3.2 grams fat, 0.3 grams saturated fat, 0.9 grams polyunsaturated fat, 1.7 grams monounsaturated fat, 4 grams protein, 23 grams carbohydrate, 2.3 grams fiber, 26 mg cholesterol, 78 mg sodium, 106 mg potassium

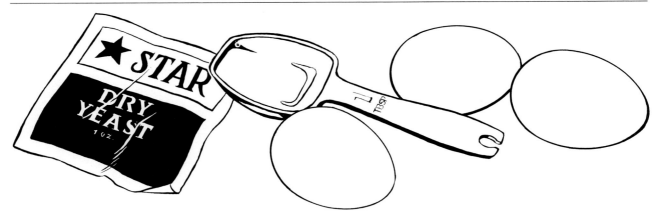

Shrimp Curry
Trinidad

Servings: 6

Pass a bowlful of chutney when you enjoy this curry. You will also want rice or pasta to soak up any extra sauce.

1 tbs. olive oil
1 cup onion, chopped
2 cloves garlic, minced
1 tsp. fresh ginger root, peeled, minced
1 (28 ozs.) can whole tomatoes, peeled

1 tbs. curry powder
½ tsp. red pepper flakes
½ tsp. salt
1 lb. large shrimp, raw, shelled
2 tbs. fresh lime juice **or** lemon juice

In a large skillet, sauté onion in oil. When soft, add garlic, ginger, tomatoes, curry, pepper and salt. Bring to a boil; stirring constantly, cook until liquid is reduced and sauce has body, about 5 minutes. Reduce heat to simmer. Add shrimp, cover and cook 4 to 5 minutes until shrimp just turn pink. Stir in lime juice and serve immediately.

Nutritional information per serving   68 calories, 2.9 grams fat, 0.4 grams saturated fat, 0.4 grams polyunsaturated fat, 1.8 grams monounsaturated fat, 3 grams protein, 10 grams carbohydrate, 1.9 grams fiber, 7 mg cholesterol, 403 mg sodium, 393 mg potassium

Tropical Fruit Cup

Brazil

In Brazil, fresh fruit cup appears on the breakfast buffet as well as the dinner dessert menu. Brazilians cut the fruits into small pieces; I prefer bite-sized chunks. Any way you fix it is the right way.

1 lb. papaya (1 medium)
½ lb. kiwi (2 large)
1 lb. orange (2 large)
1¼ lb. pineapple (¼ of a 5 lb. pineapple)

1 lb. banana (2 large)
mango, if available (optional)
toasted coconut (optional)

Peel fruits and slice or dice. If navel oranges are used, slice crosswise. If valencias are used, pare peel from orange creating a spiral; remove sections from the orange, eliminating the seeds. Toss fruits together and serve immediately, topped with coconut, if desired. The high enzyme content of these fruits causes them to digest each other on standing. Cut recipe in half in preference to saving leftovers for any extended period of time.

Nutritional information per 1-cup serving 138 calories, 0.9 grams fat, 0.1 grams saturated fat, 0.2 grams polyunsaturated fat, 0.2 grams monounsaturated fat, 2 grams protein, 35 grams carbohydrate, 4.9 grams fiber, 0 mg cholesterol, 5 mg sodium, 592 mg potassium

Index

Refried beans, 121
Rice
    Brazilian, 161
    fried, 23
Roasted chicken with
        yogurt, 146
Rolls, stuffed cabbage, 74
Rotkohl, 54
Rye bread, Swedish, 69

Salad
    black bean, 158
    Chinese chicken, 26
    Christmas, 112
    Greek, 142
    nicoise, 82
    taco, 114
    tuna vegetable, 82
Salsa fresca, 125
Salvadoran seafood stew,
        164
Sate ayam, 30
Sauce
    basil, 103
    fresh hot, 125
    lemon syrup, 48
    mock hollandaise, 85
    peanut, 33
    tomato, 110
Sauerbraten, 58
Sausage, soup with chard,
        160
Scalloped veal, Viennese,
        56
Scallops in wine sauce, 86
Schnitzel, Wiener, 56
Seafood
    red snapper Veracruz,
        126

Seafood (continued)
    Salvadoran stew, 164
    scallops in wine sauce,
        86
    shellfish in papaya
        boats, 162
    shrimp curry, 168
    tuna vegetable salad, 82
Shellfish in papaya boats,
        162
Shish kebab, 148
Shrimp curry, 168
Sicilian cheesecake, 108
Skewered
    chicken, 30
    lamb, grilled, 148
Soup
    bean and noodle, 94
    chard with sausage, 160
    cold tomato, 157
    egg and lemon, 140
    French onion, 80
    peanut millet, 8
    sour and hot, 24
    summer's here
        vegetable, 72
Soupa avgolemono, 140
Sour and hot soup, 24
Spaetzle, 64
Spiced
    basmati rice, 144
    honey bars, 62
Spicy Thai noodles, 34
Spread
    avocado, 118
    eggplant, 136
    garbanzo bean, 133
Steamed semolina, 12

Stew
    lamb and green bean, 16
    meat and vegetable with
        semolina, 10
    rabbit, 40
    Salvadoran seafood, 164
Stroganov, beef, 76
Stuffed
    cabbage rolls, 74
    grape leaves, 134
Summer's here vegetable
        soup, 72
Super tostada, 128
Swedish
    rye bread, 69
Sweet and sour
    cabbage, 54
    pork, 36
Sweet bread, Portuguese,
        166
Syrup, lemon, 48

Taco salad, 114
Tandoori murghi, 146
Tomato
    sauce, 110
    soup, 157
Tostada
    de lujo, 128
    super, 128
Tropical fruit cup, 169
Tuna vegetable salad, 82
Turkey
    stuffed cabbage rolls,
        74
Turnover, cheese-filled,
        104

Twice-baked cookies, 106

Veal, Viennese scalloped,
        56
Vegetable
    asparagus with
        hollandaise, 84
    cold tomato soup, 157
    eggplant dip, 136
    eggplant Parmesan, 96
    French onion soup, 80
    Greek salad, 142
    lamb and green bean
        stew, 16
    marinated Brussels
        sprouts, 53
    mashed potatoes and
        cabbage, 39
    poor man's caviar, 70
    soup, summer's here,
        72
    stewed okra, 15
    sweet and sour
        cabbage, 54
    tuna vegetable salad, 82
Viennese scalloped veal,
        56

Wiener schnitzel, 56

Yogurt
    cheese, 46
    with roasted chicken,
        146